Manage Like a Mother

ENDORSEMENTS

When my husband JJ and I started a family, I made the important decision to stay home with our children. Once I was ready to reenter the workforce, the fourteen-year gap in my work experience created a strike against me. Despite my vast experience, I was unable to find a company willing to take a gamble on me.

I was driven to succeed, and JJ recognized my talent and drive, so the two of us invested in founding a business built on my leadership skills. Along with a team of amazing women who also demonstrate strong leadership skills gained through mothering, we have grown Magical Vacation Planner into a successful agency.

In *Manage Like a Mother*, Valerie Cockerell reveals the leadership skills and wisdom gained through the journey of motherhood. Once you've read this book, reconsider the way you view women who are returning to the workforce. When you see the potential of mothers through the lens Valerie provides, you will discover a wealth of new leadership for your organization.

Jamie Ane Eubanks
Chief Executive Officer
Magical Vacation Planner

ICON Park is a new entertainment destination in Orlando, Florida, considered the world's most competitive market. At ICON Park, we are inspired by Dan Cockerell's *How's the Culture in Your Kingdom?* and Lee Cockerell's *Creating Magic*. We follow many of their principles and often reference these books. This has allowed us to succeed and win awards. So when I was given the chance to do an early read of Valerie Cockerell's *Manage Like a Mother*, I jumped at the opportunity. It was a great decision!

Reading this book is an outstanding, creative experience that takes the reader on a journey that we can all relate to because, as Valerie writes, "We all have a mother." She gives great leadership advice as well as insights on improving interpersonal relationships. Valerie's wisdom is based on her wealth of experience raising three children, her accomplished career at Walt Disney World, and the discernment she gained from being a consultant for businesses around the world.

The book made me think of and appreciate the ways that my mother and my wife both "managed" their children. I was thoroughly impressed by the way that Valerie describes so many of the proven tenets of successful mothering as being applicable to successful management. From the employee onboarding process to setting expectations, establishing a vision, using stories as a leadership tool, being careful to walk the talk as a role model, and creatively reducing conflict, the lessons and observations in this book are not only helping me be a better manager but also a better parent.

Christopher Jaskiewicz
President and Chief Executive Officer
ICON Park

I agree with Valerie's premise that the lessons of great leadership are transferable. And I appreciate how she has codified lessons learned and wisdom gained using thought-provoking analogies from parenting.

Many leaders—myself included—trace their core leadership lessons back to their parents, so her analogy works well. The so-called soft skills of leadership are really the hard things we execute day in and day out. Yet those skills are what differentiate great leaders, and Valerie, whom I have known for many years, models them consistently. Valerie's book celebrates and tells the stories of these critical leadership skills.

Meg Crofton
President (Retired)
Walt Disney Parks and Resorts Operations: USA and France

We can all relate to *Manage Like a Mother*, yet most of us have never taken the time to think about how parenting and leading within an organization require so many similar actions. Valerie provides a fresh nudge to remember what worked—and what didn't—in growing up and in leading.

Valerie's storytelling is perceptive. Her humble yet fun stories relate to all aspects of being a more effective team member and a leader. I would especially recommend this book to leaders at the start of their career journey.

Erin Wallace
Former Chief Operating Officer: Great Wolf Lodge
Executive Vice President of Operations: The Walt Disney
Company

Manage Like a Mother delivers a very powerful lesson in leadership. The book clearly and cleverly captures the similarities between being a mother and leading a business. The book impressively provides strong examples of growing your workforce like a mother grows a child. My daughter Cynthia is an MBA graduate with significant business experience. She is also the mother of two young children. We had plenty of positive and fun dialogue about the effective lessons learned from reading *Manage Like a Mother*. The chapters in this book provide strong, thought-provoking techniques for leading and growing a high-performance workforce. I give *Manage Like a Mother* a 5-star rating and two thumbs up.

Regynald Washington
President and Chief Executive Officer: RGW Enterprises
Former President of Dining: Paradies Lagardere
Former Morgan Stanley Portfolio Privet Equity CEO
Former Vice President: Walt Disney Global
Food & Beverage Operations

MANAGE LIKE A MOTHER

Leadership Lessons Drawn from
THE WISDOM OF MOM

VALERIE COCKERELL

NEW YORK

LONDON • NASHVILLE • MELBOURNE • VANCOUVER

MANAGE LIKE A MOTHER

Leadership Lessons Drawn from the Wisdom of Mom

Published in New York, New York, by Morgan James Publishing in partnership with Magic Press. Morgan James is a trademark of Morgan James, LLC. www.MorganJamesPublishing.com

Proudly distributed by Publishers Group West®

Morgan James BOGO™

A **FREE** ebook edition is available for you or a friend with the purchase of this print book.

CLEARLY SIGN YOUR NAME ABOVE

Instructions to claim your free ebook edition:
1. Visit MorganJamesBOGO.com
2. Sign your name CLEARLY in the space above
3. Complete the form and submit a photo of this entire page
4. You or your friend can download the ebook to your preferred device

ISBN 9781636981291 paperback
ISBN 9781636981307 ebook
Library of Congress Control Number:
2023930493

Cover and Interior Design by:
Chris Treccani
www.3dogcreative.net

Morgan James PUBLISHING
Builds with... **Habitat for Humanity™** Peninsula and Greater Williamsburg

Morgan James is a proud partner of Habitat for Humanity Peninsula and Greater Williamsburg. Partners in building since 2006.

Get involved today! Visit: www.morgan-james-publishing.com/giving-back

To Anna,
the best mom I could have hoped for.
You amaze me every day
with your talents, resilience, and joie de vivre.

TABLE OF CONTENTS

FOREWORD

There are two things mothers tend to worry about and focus on for their children: safety and education. It should be exactly the same for leaders in any organization. Your main responsibility as a leader is to produce more leaders who can go out into the world and make a positive contribution to their organizations and society.

In *Manage Like a Mother*, Valerie Cockerell clearly shows the important parallels between a mother's leadership responsibilities and those of organizational leaders.

Whether you're a man or a woman, you can become a better leader by remembering the important lessons your mother taught you. (Fathers, of course, also have a huge influence on developing their children, but as we all know, managing and leading like a mother is in a whole different category.)

Your mother led so well because she loved you and wanted you to have a happy and successful life. In the same way, you should lead well too because you respect and care about your team, wanting them to be happy and successful as well.

My mother was an expert at being clear about her expectations for me and my brother, Jerry. She was candid and consistent. One time, when we were not home by our curfew, she did not wait for us to come home. At 11:00 p.m., Mom got in her car and headed out into our little town to look for Jerry and me. Imagine the embarrassment when she found us with our friends, corralled us, and we headed home. The ride home was . . . shall we say, memorable? Never again did we fail to meet Mom's expectations. Jerry and I knew Mom cared about our safety, and that night she educated us about the importance of following through on our commitments.

We are all who we are because of the lessons our parents, grandparents, and other role models taught us—or neglected to teach us. Those lessons include empathy and disciple, fairness and firmness, appreciation and recognition, encouragement, clarity of communication, ethical behavior, respect for all people, and countless other valuable lessons and practices that enhance our lives and the lives of everyone we come into contact with.

As a leader, your people are your brand. Investing the time to learn from what Valerie has to say as a mother and a seasoned, international business leader is a worthy investment in your leadership and your people.

Lee Cockerell
Executive Vice President Walt Disney World
(Retired & Inspired)
Author of *Creating Magic: 10 Common Sense Leadership Strategies from a Life at Disney*
Proud Father-in-Law of Valerie Cockerell

HOW IT ALL STARTED

A laundromat isn't exactly the most romantic place in the world, but that is where I met my husband, Dan. It was 1991, and we were both living in Orlando, a city with no shortage of Pixie Dust. But as fate would have it, it was at a lackluster laundromat that I met my Prince Charming.

I was born and raised in Lyon, France, and I had been recruited by Disney to work in retail operations and run merchandise locations at the soon-to-open Disneyland Paris. This required me to go to Florida and learn the intricacies of Disney's retail merchandising.

At the time of our first encounter, Dan was in a management training program and had been assigned to the task force that would eventually be sent to France to support the opening of Disneyland Paris. So it was that we were both in training at Walt Disney World.

Though Dan and I met over a pile of dirty socks, our instant chemistry made our meeting far more magical. That encounter translated into a long-term relationship and a marriage of twenty-nine years and counting, one that would take us back and forth across the Atlantic.

By the end of 1991, I was back in France, joining the 12,000 Disneyland Paris cast members (Disney's term for employees) who were prepping for the opening. Dan flew to France in January

1992 with an eighteen-month visa in hand. He was to oversee the parking lot operations in preparation for the grand opening scheduled for April 12, 1992.

Our careers with Disney flourished, as did our relationship. After eighteen months of dating, we tied the knot during a very small ceremony on the outskirts of Paris. Our beautiful baby boy, Jullian, was born in Paris about two years later.

Dan and I ended up staying in France for five years before relocating to Orlando to join the team at Walt Disney World. That's where our daughter, Margot, was born in 1998, and our youngest son, Tristan, in 2001. Our family of five happily settled down in Florida with the Magic Kingdom in our backyard.

Over the next twenty years, I transitioned in and out of the workforce several times as I split my time between raising our kids and trying to pursue a career.

As we rose through the ranks, we learned a lot about Disney, but we learned even more about ourselves and about the challenges of working with people from different cultures—not to mention being married to one.

Dan eventually served as the Vice President of Epcot, Hollywood Studios, and the Magic Kingdom with its 12,000 cast members. After nine years in that role, he left Disney in 2018 to start a consulting company specializing in customer service, organizational culture, and leadership.

This change coincided with us becoming empty nesters, so it did not take long for me to join him in his new venture, drawing on my experience as a facilitator for the Disney Institute and as a leader in retail merchandising.

We started helping organizations in the US and abroad, and we were happy to discover that there indeed *is* life outside Walt Disney World.

Nowadays, Dan and I consult with organizations of all sizes in a variety of industries. Above all, we finally have the luxury to step back and reflect upon our journey. We have realized how far we have come and how much we have learned along the way.

We were fortunate to work for Disney, one of the most admired Fortune 500 companies and one of the most creative and innovative organizations that has ever existed. We learned how to lead teams to deliver outstanding customer service and exceed guest expectations in a relentless search for excellence. However, I realize now that much of my learning came from an entirely different job, one that came with neither a career path nor an instruction manual: parenting.

Along the way, I found myself drawing upon my experience as a mother to illustrate some of the leadership insights I was hoping to share. "Manage like a mother" became my go-to slogan.

My father-in-law, Lee—a sought-after keynote speaker and an accomplished leader—often shared how his mother was the source of many of the most valuable leadership lessons he has learned throughout his life. The comparison between parenting and leadership has never failed to generate understanding nods from both our audiences.

So I started to dig deeper into this analogy and found much commonality between what it takes to be a great leader and what a good mother does. I realized that parenting skills were transferable to my career. The principles that helped me train, recognize, coach, and empower teams were no different from the ones I used to raise my kids.

I found that children unwittingly help us write the playbook on leadership—so much so that the premise of this book took shape in my mind. So in the chapters that follow, you'll find insights gathered from my experience not only as a leader but also as a mother.

One more thing. Motherhood is a great source of inspiration for outstanding leadership traits and behaviors, but **you don't have to be a mother to benefit from a mother's wisdom.**

When I suggest you "manage like a mother," I'm addressing *all* leaders, no matter your gender or parental status.

After all, we all share one common denominator: **We all *have* a mother.** We've all been on the receiving end of parenting. Looking back, we know what was effective and what wasn't. And while mothers don't always do things right, we can also learn from those mistakes.

———

While I may have worked at Disney's world of make-believe for fifteen years, you will not find any magical recipes on these pages. Great leadership requires hard work, not magic. And the basic principles of leadership line up with what a mother does day in and day out.

This may seem simplistic, but if I have learned anything in my career, it's that we often look for complicated solutions when the answers are, in fact, quite simple. That's why in my work as a consultant, I often tell my clients that leadership isn't rocket science.

However, we should not assume that simple things are easy because effective leadership and effective parenting are both long-term commitments that require consistency.

Of course, I don't presume to be a perfect parent, nor am I a perfect leader. From the stories I'll share, you'll see that I haven't always made the right decisions in either role. But if we learn from our mistakes, we grow. And in the years of being a mother and a corporate leader, **I've grown not *despite* my mistakes but *because* of them.**

I've been inspired not only by my life lessons but also by watching many other moms I know well—including my mother, Anna. All of them are Wonder Women in their own right with imperfections and shortcomings, but always with good intent.

Watching mothers over many years and assessing my own mistakes brought me clarity and understanding of what works and what doesn't. I believe the following chapters will help you do the same.

———

Throughout this book, I have offered some questions that may illuminate blind spots in your leadership practices. I compiled those at the end of the book along with a few others, calling it "Over to You." You may choose to use this section to guide you in applying a mother's wisdom to your role as a leader.

One last thing. You will find quotes sprinkled throughout this book that I have collected from friends and relatives from around the world—words of wisdom and advice that their mothers shared with them as they grew up. These quotes don't always tie in with the content of the chapter, but they demonstrate that no matter their age, nationality, or culture, moms never fail to share their powerful insights in their own special way.

PART 1

Laying the Foundation for Success

1
Character Matters

———

Eighteen months into our marriage, Dan and I traveled to New York City for a long weekend. It was November 1994. While in the city, we went to have some drinks at the Peacock Alley Bar at the Waldorf Astoria. This was no coincidence. My father-in-law, Lee, had debuted his career at the Waldorf as a banquet server in the early sixties. He had shared with us the story behind the bar's name and recommended we check it out.

During the 1920s, the Waldorf and the Astoria were two separate hotels connected by a long promenade where the bar was located. This exclusive venue attracted the rich and powerful. It also drew many young women who would parade from the Waldorf to the Astoria hoping to catch the eye of a wealthy patron. Hence the name, Peacock Alley.

While sipping drinks, our conversation drifted toward the question of expanding our family. Dan and I had vaguely broached the subject before, but this time we found ourselves doing a detailed comparison of our views on parenting. We discussed our respective approaches to child-rearing, be it in regard to education, childcare, culture, or the values we hoped to impart to our children. Not surprisingly, we were aligned on all fronts.

It was important to both of us that our children be exposed to French and American culture, and that they were to be given a well-rounded education as well as an opportunity to discover their talents and skills unburdened by parental expectations.

We also had a shared view on parental duties, disciplinary tactics, and religious education. I was thrilled to hear Dan express a true commitment to gender equality and voice his desire to become a whole-hearted partner in sharing all parental duties.

We discussed our respective levels of involvement, the kind of childcare we wanted our kids to enjoy, as well as the financial implications of expanding our family. We both hoped to have more than one child, though we did not settle on a specific number. We also agreed on the timeline and decided to put our plan in motion right away.

> *"Women have many faults. Men have only two: Everything they say and everything they do."*
> Ella to Priscilla
> Ardmore, OK, USA

We left the Peacock Alley with a shared vision of our future family unit. On our way back to our hotel, Dan joked that should we have a boy, he would be called Waldorf, and a girl would be named Astoria.

Fortunately, he had forgotten all about that idea when Jullian was born ten months later.

———

How does this relate to leadership? you may wonder.

For the most part—at least in Western cultures—women have a say about their life partner. They get to choose whom they will start a family with. They ensure that their partner's values and approach to parenting are aligned with their own. They also look for someone willing to learn and adapt along with them, as no one can be fully prepared for life's changes—especially those brought on by having a baby.

As a leader, I've always kept these basic principles front and center when hiring new people for my team. Much like I made sure my husband and I saw eye to eye on how we would raise our children, I hired people who share my work ethic, mindset, and values.

Skills matter, of course, in some professions more than in others. (Would you want a pilot with great skills or one with great values?) In most cases, I would rather hire someone whose values align with mine than someone with the full set of skills.

Skills can be improved with time, training, and experience. Values, on the other hand, are deeply ingrained and hardly malleable.

As a leader, you may be able to help an employee shift *slightly* to align their values with that of your team, but you cannot expect to fundamentally change someone's character. And in the end, what forms the glue of your organization is the consensus regarding which behaviors are deemed acceptable and which are unacceptable. This determines your ability to successfully lead a team with diverse skills and personalities toward the same destination.

This is why I've always looked at values and attitude as nonnegotiable. Even when told that we just needed someone able to do the job—the proverbial warm body to fill a spot—I wouldn't budge on this.

When *one* employee has different values from the rest of the team, it shows. It affects the team culture and impacts the recruit's ability to succeed, not to mention the productivity and morale of the rest of the employees. This becomes contagious. Before you know it, you have a dysfunctional organization.

When given the choice, **always prioritize values, ethics, and mindset over skills, experience, and knowledge**. This must be the most important consideration throughout your entire selection process.

As a future mother, you and your partner discuss your views on parenting *before* starting a family. You ensure your values are aligned and your approaches are the same. When selecting a team, you must do the same to avoid potential trouble later on.

"Figure out what you want to do and who you want to share the journey with."
Margaret Winifred to Jeanne
Durango, CO, USA

2
Welcome Aboard

———

Paris, August 1995. I was eight months into my first pregnancy and happily waddling from my house to the local aquatic center to swim my daily laps when I bumped into a friend of mine (no pun intended). She was also pregnant and nearing her due date. We both looked like we could pop at any time. I suspect the teenage lifeguard was praying that neither my friend nor I would go into labor during his shift.

Because Dan and I were living in France at the time, I was eligible for two months of maternity leave leading up to my due date, and another three months beyond that. Five months of bliss . . . or so I thought.

After exchanging pleasantries, my friend shared *in detail* all the purchases she and her husband had made and all they had done to prepare for the arrival of their firstborn. Military campaigns or moon explorations would have paled in comparison! Their preparations included stocking up on baby supplies, attending Lamaze classes, finding a suitable pediatrician, identifying and interviewing a reliable babysitter, looking into potential daycare options, conducting nanny interviews, and on and on.

I listened and nodded politely, excusing myself after a while so I could go about my usual swim routine. While doing laps, I could not get the conversation off my mind. The more I thought about all she shared, the more dreadful the realization: I was a few weeks away from delivery, and I was woefully unprepared. Panic set in.

"Never look for perfection from your friends."
Emily to Suzie
Boston, MA, USA

I naively thought I could rely on the sheer power of my untested maternal instinct to face whatever challenges may lay ahead. Was I underestimating how much our way of life was about to change?

That evening, I frantically scavenged books and magazines in search of information so Dan and I could formulate a plan of attack. I made a long list of supplies and an even longer to-do list.

In the weeks that followed, I attended classes and peppered all the mothers I knew with questions—friends and relatives, experienced moms, and freshly minted ones. Of course, each one of them had a ton of recommendations, and my list of must-haves grew accordingly. I learned all I could hope for and then some.

I lined up my support system of friends, parents, and in-laws, not to mention a nanny and a trusted pediatrician. And in addition to painting the nursery, Dan and I purchased all the baby supplies known to mothers, including a crib, bottles, diapers, formula, some plush toys and rattles, a colorful mobile, and a nightlight. We chose the baby announcements and built an impressive list of numbers to put on speed dial for all the what-ifs and possible hiccups.

When the time came, we were ready. Dan drove me to the maternity hospital at about 1 a.m. on September 2, and our beautiful baby boy, Jullian, was born a short five hours later. In all, it was as smooth a delivery as one could hope for.

I thought that the most challenging part of the job was done, but I would soon be proven wrong. The hard work had just begun. There would be many more questions to answer and skills to master. However, at that very moment, we were confident we had thoroughly prepared for our first child's "onboarding."

———

Starting a new job may not bring as dramatic a lifestyle change as becoming a parent does, but some of the very principles of a successful transition into parenthood certainly apply in the work environment.

As I mentioned earlier, I have transferred in and out of the workforce several times. I have experienced multiple first days on the job, facilitated some as a leader, and learned how a variety of organizations approach onboarding.

Some companies' processes are flawless. Others? Not so much. Here's what I've found regarding what makes for great onboarding.

First Impressions Matter

Prepare for your new hires with the same thoughtfulness you'd prepare for a baby's arrival. The experience of someone's first day at a company is critical. It foreshadows how much you as a leader are willing to invest in your team members. Put yourself in the shoes of the new hires arriving full of hopes and with a ton of enthusiasm. *What do you notice? Does it look like your organization cares about them? Are the new hires' arrival a priority? Are you making the recruits feel welcome?*

As a leader, don't underestimate the impact of this first day. It tells a story about what you stand for, if the organization is willing to invest in its employees, and what kind of leaders oversee the operations. **Onboarding provides a window into the heart of your business.**

"Impressions matter. Dress for success."

Kay to Holli

Brecksville, OH, USA

Consider the first things they will experience. Regrettably, I have seen some companies take their staff to a sticky table at the back of a gloomy cafeteria to fill out mountains of paperwork as a first—and sometimes only—step to onboarding. But I have also seen companies take recruits to training rooms with overstuffed leather chairs, flowers, and well-stocked buffets.

Be Picky About Who Facilitates Onboarding

On day one at Disney, they put every new hire—regardless of position—through a class called Traditions. Everyone comes out of that class thoroughly covered in Pixie Dust.

People are often surprised to find out that this class is facilitated by a rotating roster of frontline employees. These folks' enthusiasm, passion for the organization, and energy are not only genuine but also highly contagious precisely because they're frontline employees.

The first encounter with whoever is assigned to be your gatekeeper of sorts will either leave a lasting positive impression on your new hire or an indelible stain on your company's reputation.

Introduce Your New Hire to Their Work Environment

Where appropriate, make sure new hires are given a tour of the facilities, including the parking lot, restrooms, and cafeteria.

If not, you may find them wandering around not sure how they can get to where they need to be. So introduce them to their new surroundings. Provide a map if it would help.

This step may seem obvious, but you'd be surprised to see how many organizations expect recruits to figure this out by themselves. Even at Disney, I would sometimes come across a new cast member wandering around the Magic Kingdom's tunnel (also known as the Utilidor) in search of the elusive cafeteria.

If relevant, you should identify the new hire's workspace, which should be clean and welcoming, and you should provide all office essentials, including name tags, passwords, and login details.

Also, don't forget to explain the safety protocol and point out the different departments and their functions. Many companies simply hand newcomers an organizational chart full of names and titles that doesn't serve much purpose other than helping them see the lines of reporting.

Make sure a new hire understands who's responsible for what. This turns an org chart into a roadmap so they can find support when they need answers, much like a night-light provides comfort to a child.

Assign an Onboarding Buddy

Speaking of helping them find answers, assigning a mentor to help new hires navigate their first few months at your organization can make all the difference in the world. In their first days on the job, new hires often go through a whirlwind of meet-and-greets with colleagues. All of this can be quite overwhelming.

If your company has several departments, understanding everyone's contribution and their respective roles can be hard. To make things worse, organizations operate and change at breakneck speed—especially in the service industry and the tech world—and this is enough to give a new employee corporate whiplash.

*"To be successful, it is not **what** you know, it is **who** you know."*
Kay to Holli
Brecksville, OH, USA

Think of the onboarding buddy as bringing the sense of security that new hires crave. Having someone they can turn to with questions can provide the comfort and the familiarity they need during this transition time, much like a special bear or blanket does to a child.

Make Sure They Know It's OK to Ask Questions

One of the first investments a new mother makes is a baby monitor so she can know when the baby needs her. Think about this for a second: *Where is the baby monitor for your employees?*

Sometimes we tell them we are here for them but fail to provide them with the opportunity to ask questions, or we keep our office door closed. So tell them on day one that it is OK for them to ask questions—*any* questions. And then, check in on them regularly and make yourself available.

Send Out an Announcement

Much like you'd do for a newborn, let everyone in your company know about your new hire's arrival, what their role will be, along with some personal and career information. This will allow your team to connect with them and create rapport.

Go Meet Them

If all of the onboarding is taken care of by other staff members, make sure you personally go and greet your new hires. This will show them how important they are to your organization. More than just going to shake their hand, get to know them personally. Ask questions—lots of them.

Get to know where they're from, where they studied, and what they like to do in their spare time. Are they married? Do they have kids? If so, what kind of childcare arrangement do they have? Go beyond the obvious. Know how they get to work every day and how long their commute takes. After all, their life at home overlaps with their life at work. All of this impacts their ability to be effective.

The time you spend getting to know them is an investment that will pay long-term dividends. It sends a powerful message that you care about your team members and that you want them to be successful.

———

Building an efficient onboarding process is like providing the type of hypercare that you'd provide a newborn. The idea is to make them feel valued, celebrated, safe, and—dare I say—loved.

Your new hires are on an emotional high having just landed the job. They are also nervous about starting in their new work environment. It may even be their first job. What they experience at this point is a mixture of enthusiasm and anxiety.

Your responsibility as a leader is to ensure a great integration by calming their nerves while sustaining their level of enthusiasm. This is the first of many stepping stones in the bonding process.

If you've done that effectively, your new hire will be going home at the end of their first day excited about the days to come and looking forward to coming back and starting their training.

3
Teach Them Their ABCs

———

From day one, new parents are faced with many unanswered questions. *How do I know if my baby has eaten enough? Is it time to introduce new food to their diet? How long should I let them cry?* In my case, there were also some pretty basic questions like, *How do I change a diaper?!*

Admittingly, as my firstborn, Jullian was the first baby whose diaper I ever had to change. I quickly found out that it wasn't a task for the faint of heart. Though I briefly considered wearing a hazmat suit at some point, I finally mastered the skill after many failed attempts that resulted in unnecessary loads of laundry. Today, I can probably change a diaper one-handed and with my eyes closed.

Still, I had so much more to learn and had many questions.

In theory, I had gleaned a lot of answers from all the mothers I had consulted with. But *hearing* how to care for a newborn is one thing. Having the confidence to do it by myself is another challenge altogether. All the wisdom that my friends had imparted seemed to evaporate the moment Jullian uttered his first cry.

Fortunately, the French healthcare system provides new mothers with a week-long hospital stay—at least, they did back then. For the first couple of days, the new mom gets to simply rest. Then, little by little, her contribution increases at a pace that suits her. If she so chooses, she can watch as her baby receives their first bath. Once she's ready to bathe the baby herself, she can do so, either under the watchful eye of a nurse or independently.

It's entirely up to the mother to decide when she's ready to do tasks like this by herself.

Beyond that initial help, French parents are also afforded wonderful support and resources. A pediatric adviser came to our house to ensure it was baby proofed and provided us with last-minute recommendations and advice. It was like we were given our very own baby whisperer. Plus, I was given access to a baby hotline, where my questions would be answered any time, day or night.

Despite all the support I had access to, it didn't take long for me to be emotionally spent, not to mention being in dire need of a decent night's sleep. So I was thrilled when my parents, Anna and Victor, came to visit us in Paris. I benefited from my mom's experience and her calming presence. She gladly took over some of the baby duties, providing me with some precious time to take a nap or indulge in a hot bath, not to mention expertly answering all my questions.

"When you become a new mom, make sure you shower, get dressed, and go outside to get fresh air every day!"
Marcy to Lisa
New York, NY, USA

And after my parents left, my in-laws, Lee and Priscilla, arrived from the US to meet Jullian and give us a hand in caring for him. When Dan and I were baffled by Jullian's 5 to 7 p.m. crying fits—often referred to as a baby's witching hour—Lee and Priscilla came to the rescue, walking around the house with Jullian in their arms until he finally calmed down. They also knew just how to remedy a diaper rash or a tummy ache, and they could rock the baby to sleep in five minutes flat.

The point is, we had a *lot* of support, and everyone was ready to make themselves available at a moment's notice. Dan and I were soon totally convinced that it indeed takes a village to raise a child. But we mostly realized how fortunate we were to have access to so many resources. It gave us confidence in our new role as parents and the reassurance that everything was going to be OK.

———

Much like new parents, new hires need to be trained. They also need to be encouraged, reassured, and supported. They need to be given time to digest and internalize the mountain of information coming their way.

Well-intentioned organizations often provide their new employees with a manual filled with standard operating procedures that lists all there is to know about their new role. This is the workplace version of *What to Expect When You're Expecting,* guaranteed to be found on every new mother's nightstand. However, working through a staff manual can be like drinking from a fire hose and the data overload often leaves a new hire overwhelmed.

Much like new mothers, each new hire masters the skills needed for the job at their own pace, and that is OK. We all have different learning styles.

My kids, for instance, all learned how to ride a bike without training wheels in a different way.

Jullian sang out loud to steady his nerves and help him focus on riding in a straight line. Margot, on the other hand, screamed, "Don't let go!" at the top of her lungs long after I *had* let go. And when Tristan first tried riding a bike, he decided it was pointless, threw the bike to the side, ignored it for a few weeks, and then one day, he just jumped on and took off all by himself.

The same goes for your team. They all learn and process information at different paces and in different ways. Some have to see it, some have to hear it, and others have to do it. Others need to do all three.

Here's what I've found regarding what makes for a good training program.

Incorporate Different Learning Styles

When it comes to new hires, you won't know which method will be most effective for them. So your training program should cover hearing, seeing, *and* doing.

While you can start by teaching the knowledge and skills verbally, *do not* stop there. Instead, provide trainees with an opportunity to watch others in action. The ideal program will then team up new hires with seasoned mentors under whose supervision they can perform the task for however long is necessary, before they are launched to work independently.

You may think this is excessive, but keep in mind that you have already invested both time and resources in hiring and selecting your new hires. You might as well ensure that they are trained properly so they can contribute to the success of your team.

Encourage, Guide, and Coach

Granted, new hires will make mistakes along the way, but as a leader, you should celebrate efforts and even small amounts of progress regardless of mistakes made.

This is almost like teaching a child how to walk, one of the rites of passage that brings parents both joy and a broken back as you guide the little one, holding both their hands to provide balance.

The moment a child attempts their first steps on their own, we cheer their efforts but also offer words of comfort when they inevitably lose their balance and come crashing on their rear end.

Every step is celebrated, every milestone applauded, and every cry soothed so that we can restore the confidence the toddler needs to try again.

The same goes for potty training. I have heard many stories about how parents approach this dreaded task, all revolving around an outpour of encouragement and rewards. Dan and I, for example, would promptly break into what we called the "poopy dance" whenever a sitting session had been productive.

While you won't need to use the same amount of coaxing and coddling with new hires, they do need encouragement, guidance, and coaching. They will also need positive reinforcement and redirection when they veer off track.

> *"Give it a shot anyway.*
> *What will be, will be!"*
> Marceline to Anna
> Ambérieu-en-Bugey, France

Like all new parents, it took Dan and me time to learn all we needed to know about parenting. Likewise, new hires must understand that they don't need to know all the answers right from the start, that you expect them to make mistakes, and that they're surrounded by the proverbial village willing to help.

They Don't Know What They Don't Know

Most companies have training schedules that leave little wiggle room for adjustment. But here's a caveat: New hires want to make a good first impression. When probed, they may be reluctant to admit that they need more time or that they still have questions. At the same time, you may encounter some who are overconfident, thinking they know more than they do.

We've all been there, those early days on a job when we don't know what we don't know . . . yet. Just like we didn't always know which questions to ask, neither do our new employees.

When our kids turned fifteen, along came the dreaded time for them to get a learner's permit. Schools in our area didn't offer driver's ed, and Dan and I came up with many excuses to delay the inevitable. We even created prerequisites such as, "You can learn how to operate a car once you've mastered operating the dishwasher and the washing machine!"

No matter how hard we tried, we eventually had to face the music and teach our kids to drive. Dan conveniently deferred to *moi*. I was reluctant to do this and objected on account of being French—French drivers are notoriously wild and reckless. However, someone had to do it, so I eventually gave in simply because I knew my car was safer than Dan's.

I identified the best route around the neighborhood, following Amazon and UPS's example by limiting the number of left turns, the cause of many accidents. I also considered the best time of day to train the new driver—early Saturday and Sunday mornings being by far the quietest.

This is how it came to be that my teenagers and I would tour the neighborhood at 6 a.m. every weekend, almost always circling the area clockwise until they mastered the basic driving skills and calmed their nerves (and mine) enough for them to hop onto bigger roads and face more traffic.

Along the way, I would remind them that driving a car was easy. Having to anticipate what other drivers were going to do and dodge their moves? That was an entirely different proposition. That's the part that drivers simply don't know.

My words elicited some eye-rolling from my kids, no doubt, until Tristan learned this lesson the hard way. One day, some guy came shooting out of a side street and cut in front of us, oblivious to our presence. Tristan swerved into the opposite lane and narrowly—quite miraculously—avoided hitting oncoming traffic.

When Tristan finally pulled over, we all exhaled a sigh of relief. Everyone on board had a whole new understanding of what I meant by, "You don't know what you don't know!"

My point is this: When planning training of any kind, it's best to think about the environment and the pressure your trainees will be exposed to, not to mention assessing all possible liabilities. You wouldn't expect your teenage kids to drive on a highway during rush hour on day one, so why would you send your new hires into the fray where the risks are the highest?

Instead of sending a new hire into the proverbial baptism by fire, test their knowledge by asking them appropriate questions and assessing their skills during off-peak hours or away from big projects.

Evaluate their preparedness objectively and without judgment or pressure. Give them an opportunity to get started in a stress-free environment, then ramp up the pressure as they master the skills they need. Most of all, make sure they're comfortable requesting more time if that's what they need.

Learn from New Hires

On a side note, also keep your ears open, because you can learn a lot from new hires if you pay attention to their insights. They have fresh eyes, and you should want to leverage their point of view and tap into the observations that sprout from their first few weeks with your company.

Creativity and innovation often stem from random ideas (more on that later), and what may at first seem like a naive or preposterous suggestion may turn into a real gem of an idea.

Check In on Them

Finally, create a checkpoint for new hires about three months after onboarding. By then, they will have had time to settle down and reflect on the information, supplies, and knowledge that was shared with them during training. They will be able to give you feedback on what they were provided versus what they *wish* they'd been given.

Ask them questions such as: *What roadblocks have you encountered? What do you wish you had known about the job? Is there an area you wish you'd known more about? What could we do differently as an organization? How can we better prepare for future new hires? Who and what was most helpful through your onboarding and training process?*

Learning from their insights can help you improve your organization's training program and ensure greater effectiveness from your recruits.

———

The amount of effort you put into tailoring your training program for your new hires—including answering their questions and providing the support they need—demonstrates that as a leader and an organization, you're setting a recruit up for long-term success, not just filling in a vacant position.

Your commitment to the best training also shows that you recognize their individual needs as employees. This foreshadows the type of relationship you will be able to build from that point on—one based on mutual respect and understanding.

4
You've Got a Friend in Me

———

Years ago, my mother-in-law, Priscilla, gave me a needlepoint pillow that said, "Discover wildlife: Have children." Boy, was that an understatement!

In case you don't know, during their formative years, toddlers experience rapid mood swings, and in just a couple of minutes, the happy-go-lucky child becomes utterly unreasonable and an obstinate little . . . oh, never mind.

Nothing could have prepared me for the temper tantrums of the terrible twos. Jullian had his share of moments, and once I figured out what triggered his temper and learned to control it, I naively thought I knew everything there was to know about raising kids.

And then came Margot, and out the window went the playbook. Margot managed to stretch this phase into her terrible threes *and* fours with me being none the wiser as to what was the root cause. (Let me reassure you: Our daughter is now a terrific young woman who's perfectly well-mannered, but back then, civility was but a distant dream and looked like an improbable outcome.)

The reality is that, at that age, toddlers struggle to express themselves due to their limited language skills. And as they become more independent, they resent having to rely on their parents to get some tasks done. They also get frustrated at having little say in the decision-making process, and they generally struggle to comprehend the impact of their actions.

More importantly, toddlers do not know how to manage their emotions, and they're ill-equipped to deal with stress. As a result, to blow off steam they tend to vocalize, preferably at the top of their lungs.

When it came to vocalizing, Margot had power *and* range. She exhausted our patience with her ear-splitting deliveries. I attempted to curb her tantrums with all manner of strategies: I alternately ignored her, tried to console her, reasoned with her, threatened her, or attempted to negotiate with her. *Nothing* worked. Not even when I once spanked her little behind. (We were in France at the time and no one there would give you the stink eye, much less charge you with child abuse.) But even a spanking failed to yield any results.

So, what to do? French women like to theorize that wine was invented with this very situation in mind so that mothers could indulge in "self-care" to survive child-rearing. Joking aside, it takes time and commitment to get to know your children so you can adjust your parenting style and customize your approach to their needs and personality.

It only took a few tantrums for me to realize that I could not deal with Margot the way I dealt with Jullian. Later on, I discovered that Tristan too required a different playbook. I found out that **much of the success of parenting is contingent on your ability to get to know each child individually and understand how they operate.**

When it came to Margot, I was determined to find the source of her frustration. At first, I assumed she was simply tired. But then I noticed that these tantrums were taking place at random times—sometimes in the early morning or right after naptime.

Then I considered what she was eating. Too much sugar? Not enough food? Curbing her sugar intake or trying to feed her did not help either.

I wondered whether she was overwhelmed by too much stimulation or maybe too much socializing. No such luck with that either.

I studied Margot's behaviors, listened intently to what she would say, even casually, and made a mental list of what stimulated her and what depleted her energy. I finally figured out what triggered her tantrums: a lack of order.

Margot did much better when her days were structured. Surprises and a change in her daily rhythm threw her off. She needed to know how the day would play out, and she thrived on routine. This became abundantly clear once she started preschool where her days were highly structured and she had a predictable regimen, both of which appealed to her character.

Things improved seemingly overnight because she had found her element.

Generally, mothers know what their children react to best. They pay attention to what their kids naturally gravitate to, what environment they favor, how they make decisions, and if they thrive among a group of friends or do better one-on-one—all valuable information to determine what children respond to and what helps them thrive.

You think forging great relationships with kids is hard? You bet! Mothers constantly do a delicate dance where they straddle the line between being a loving and caring mom on one side and teaching and coaching their kids with a serving of tough love on

"You'll catch more flies with honey than vinegar."
Lettie Mae to Vickie
Quitman, MS, USA

the other. If moms do this effectively, it forges a great relationship and clears the way for a peaceful household.

Understanding Margot helped me deflate her negative emotions and move well beyond tantrums to a close relationship and mutual understanding.

———

Forging great relationships with those you work with makes for high-performing teams. **Getting to know the people who work around you and understand how they operate is the best investment of time you can make as a leader.** Yet this is something that is often pushed to the back burner because many seemingly more important things fill the agenda.

Despite knowing the importance of building great relationships, leaders fail to make it a priority simply because it doesn't seem urgent. There are no financial results attached to it and no key performance indicators (KPIs) to remind them that it matters. As a result, tasks that have immediate consequences take precedence.

You might think it's OK to allow time to organically shape relationships. But knowing your team—*really* knowing them—doesn't just take time, it takes intentionality. Sometimes people spend years working together without the slightest idea as to what makes a colleague tick, how they tend to react to stress, or what their life circumstances are. This is especially true in large organizations.

Not knowing teammates makes working together more difficult and leaves a lot of room for assumptions, misinterpretations, and misunderstandings.

I cannot think of a single leadership responsibility that isn't made easier by having great relationships—communication, setting expectations, and giving recognition or feedback. So here's what leaders should try to do.

Get to Know Your Team Well—Right Away

If you understand how important this is and agree that strong relationships make work easier, why wait to work on strengthening ties with your team? Mothers know that forging a bond with a newborn is essential for shaping a mutual connection. Likewise, if you aspire to build a foundation of trust with your team members, engage immediately so that you get to know them personally.

Learn the name of their spouse or significant other and even their kids' names. Ask them about their background, including where they grew up. Find out what their favorite food, drinks, and sports teams are. Do they have food allergies or dislikes? Know what makes them tick and what worries them. Get to know their priorities, their passions, their hopes for the future, and what they see as their purpose.

Also observe and make notes of the following: *What do they need to relax and recharge? How do they arrive at decisions or reach conclusions? Are they thorough and methodical in their approach? Do they shine in group settings or tend to talk only when prompted? Do they like to be praised publicly or prefer to be acknowledged in private? How do they respond to change and last-minute requests?*

These aren't details you collect in a single sitting. Learning their preferences and understanding how they can thrive will happen gradually as you observe them in action or during one-on-one touch-base meetings and casual conversations.

Knowing your team well will help you figure out how they think, what they need to operate at their best, what they have to offer, and what throws them off track.

Share a Little About Yourself

If you talk about your family, hobbies, and passions, they will be more inclined to do the same. Just be mindful to not dominate the conversation.

You may discover common interests, similar tastes, or points of view, all of which will give you more touch points to build on going forward. You may even be able to connect them to others in the organization with similar passions and ease their integration.

> *"You can't always be the smartest person in the class, but you can be the nicest."*
> Anna Bella to Jamie Mitchell, IN, USA

Along the way, you may also identify some skills or talents that would have gone otherwise unnoticed. Jullian recently landed a job with a big bio-med engineering firm. During his onboarding, he spent a couple of hours with his direct leader, getting to know each other and going over some basic rules of engagements.

While chatting about one thing or another, his boss found out that Jullian has dual French and American citizenship and that he's fluent in French. As it turns out, the organization has a significant presence in France, and this could prove to be a very useful skill. Though it was stated on his résumé, this information had not made it past HR.

In the same way, you may never know what you'll find out just casually shooting the breeze with a new team member.

Customize Your Leadership Style

Much like mothers do, you should be able to rely on your understanding of each of your team members' personalities to adjust your leadership style. Some will require more direction, and you may have to schedule regular one-on-ones. Others may prefer working independently and will turn to you only as needed.

The introverts on your team may not contribute unless addressed directly, yet they have a wealth of ideas and an interesting perspective to contribute. You can make a point to engage them during the meeting or solicit their opinion at a later time.

Some individuals need constant encouragement or validation—some in public, and others only ever privately. You may have to find a few minutes to spare just so you can support and casually recognize them.

And when someone you thought you knew acts out of character, consider that they may be dealing with personal issues. Given the opportunity to express themselves, they may alert you to the challenges they may be facing. This will also allow you to customize your approach and adjust your expectations.

Listen with Both Ears

I recently listened to a terrific TED Talk by UCLA gymnastics coach, Valorie Kondos Field. Miss Val related how she has always kept an open-door policy and engaged in spontaneous and casual conversations with members of her team, even when these laid-back talks followed no particular agenda and were unrelated to gymnastics.

One day, team gymnast Kyla Ross showed up at the coach's office and uncharacteristically talked about an insignificant topic. Kyla was usually withdrawn, so Miss Val realized the small talk might be a roundabout way to get to a matter of importance.

She made a conscientious effort not to interrupt and gave Kyla room to articulate what was on her heart. The gymnast eventually confided that she had been a victim of Larry Nassar, the former USA Gymnastics national team doctor. Chances are that without Miss Val's listening skills, Kyla may never have shared her story.

People want to be heard, and as a leader, you must provide the channel and opportunity for team members to reach out to you and share whatever is on their minds. And it's your responsibility to create an atmosphere where your team is comfortable sharing with you and generally letting you know when the pressure is mounting or when they're struggling. They should be able to voice their frustration before it becomes unbearable.

> "The robe does not make the monk."
> Anna to Valerie
> Lyon, France

So when listening to your team members, listen deeply. Go beyond the first impression. Much like a mother does with her child, try to understand the whole person, including how they operate psychologically.

———

When you know the people you collaborate with, they'll know you care about *them,* not just about KPIs. And when your team knows that you have their back, chances are they'll blow the KPIs out of the water.

So invest the time and get to *really* know them. Your success as a leader depends on it.

5

Listening Ears and an Understanding Heart

———

I n her first few months of school, Margot once stomped into the house seething. The reason? Her teacher had told my daughter that she was having a bad hair day.

Though Margot's pigtails indeed looked disheveled, I was surprised a grown-up would say that to a child, so I empathized with her. I let her know that I, too, would be very upset had someone said that to me. That was enough to immediately diffuse Margot's anger. Her feelings had been validated.

From that point on, I used this insight. If Margot appeared distraught, I'd let her express her frustration and help her find words she could use to label her emotions. If she was scared, I'd comfort her rather than dismiss her feelings.

Sometimes, Margot would simply declare, "I'm mad." When I'd ask for a reason, she'd tell me she didn't know. So I would point out that I, too, was sometimes mad without quite knowing why. (Dan can attest to that.) Once again, knowing that I could relate was all she needed to feel better. My daughter knew she could share her emotions without being judged or dismissed, and that she was heard and understood.

On a good day, I would try to gauge how to respond when my kids had an emotional outburst or appeared upset. Before I'd react, I would ask myself, *Is this worth saying? Is this going to be effective? Is this the right time and place?* Once I knew the answers to these questions, I would try to pick the right path to defuse the situation.

Doing all this required that I demonstrated the fundamentals of emotional intelligence (EQ)—self-awareness, self-control, and empathy—things I hoped my children would emulate. And what better way to teach than by setting an example, right? Easier said than done.

Knowing that children watch their parents closely and emulate their reactions, I would try to get a hang of my own emotions before I would cross the Rubicon. Unfortunately, I wasn't always successful, especially while dealing with teenagers as problems and emotions became more complex.

Admittingly, demonstrating self-control wasn't always easy. How many times have I failed to bite my tongue before making a curt remark?

My patience was regularly tested. When we were already late getting out of the house and a reluctant toddler or teenager decided she wanted a different outfit. When I finally pulled up into the school parking lot after a grueling forty-five-minute car ride and my nine-year-old son would announce that he had forgotten to put his shoes on. When a passive-aggressive teenager would ignore my comments or questions, roll his eyes, and walk away shrugging . . .

"No matter what, always look on the bright side."
Isabelle to Elsa
Ambérieu-en-Bugey, France

There were many similar instances when my willpower failed to get the better of my French temper. Every single incident was a litmus test of my ability to practice self-awareness and self-control so I could regulate my emotions—a prerequisite for maintaining a good relationship with my children.

And as all mothers know too well, this is easy to understand but oh so hard to execute.

———

Great leaders have a high EQ. They know how to manage their emotions and how those emotions affect the people around them. Much like mothers try to validate their kids' feelings, such leaders understand others and demonstrate empathy. And in the end, they forge better relationships, ones based on trust and mutual respect.

Some of these qualities may come naturally to you. More often than not, they will require practice and commitment. Understanding the fundamentals of EQ is a good starting point.

Work on Your Self-Awareness

How often do you pause to reflect on your day, to think about how you responded to situations? Many people are oblivious to their display of emotions. They may raise their voice, interrupt others, sulk, or appear agitated without realizing it.

Mothers don't hesitate to alert children to their behavior and point out why it may be inappropriate or, worse yet, offensive. Unfortunately, leaders seldom have someone around who can call them out the way a mother does. So try some introspection.

At the end of the day, think through how you responded to events. Consider if you need to apologize to anyone. **Identify the triggers to your emotional reactions** so you can respond differently the next time around. Notice if there are patterns to how you react to difficult situations.

Asking a close friend or a relative for candid feedback is a great way to improve your self-awareness. And if possible, go ask your mom. She should be able to tell you in no uncertain terms what triggers your emotional outbursts.

Practice Self-Control

Once you know what sets you off, you can control your impulses. Not that it's that simple. Just keep in mind that self-control doesn't mean you have to remain silent. Instead, it is about **expressing emotions** *appropriately.* When under the spell of intense emotions, we've all said or done things we've regretted. So you must try to read the signs and self-regulate.

First, if you notice your heart racing, your palms getting sweaty, or your hands shaking, it is best to take a moment. You can address the issue once you've calmed down. Then, change your thought patterns and reframe the situation in a positive light.

Finally, follow a mom's advice: Take a couple of deep breaths or count to ten before you speak. Doing so takes practice, mindfulness, and—going back to step one—a whole lot of self-awareness.

Show Empathy

Finally, you need the ability to demonstrate empathy. As a leader, you cannot tell someone to feel one way or another as everyone is entitled to their own emotions. Showing empathy does not mean you should agree either. It means you **recognize the feelings of others even if you don't share them**.

When dealing with someone who is expressing their sadness, worries, or frustration, refrain from talking about yourself–even if you are just trying to justify your actions or show that you have dealt with similar circumstances. Stay away from phrases that start with *can't you just . . .* or *at least you have . . .* as doing so discounts their feelings.

You must find just the right words to appease the person you are dealing with, show that they are being heard and validate their emotions. And in doubt, a simple "I am so sorry you feel that way" will suffice.

Put EQ to Good Use

As a leader, you're bound to witness some temper tantrums—not the kind accompanied by crying fits and feet stomping, but mounting frustration that eventually leads to disengagement and ultimately turnover.

When team members cannot cope with the stress that comes with their jobs, they may become curt, irritable, and uncooperative, much like a child who is subject to overstimulation.

Life events coupled with job stress—including any tension between colleagues—can all contribute to a gradual deterioration of their performance, not to mention their health. And when you are in the middle of the fray, you can easily fail to see the warning signs.

However, if you have taken the time to get to know your collaborators, you may recognize the trigger points and address them before it is too late. You will have a mental benchmark of how they operate at their best, and you will notice when something is amiss. The red flags will allow you to intervene before these individuals reach a point of no return and either become a casualty of burnout or slam the door on their way out.

These are some of the warning signs you should be looking for: *Do you notice changes in the team member's performance and behaviors? Are they more flustered or seem more overwhelmed than usual? Do they sulk or demonstrate hostility through their body lan-*

guage? *Are they quick to present a rebuttal? Do you sense disinterest and distraction?*

If you notice any of this, it may be a good idea to engage them in what I'd call a one-on-one "stay conversation." Do a bit of investigating. Ask them what they look forward to on their way to work every morning. If no clear answer is forthcoming, you may have a problem on your hands. Ask what they are interested in learning and what skills they are hoping to build. A blank stare will tell you all you need to know about their plans within the organization.

Take a leap and investigate further: *Have you ever considered leaving the organization and if so, what prompted it? Did this happen recently? Is your workload manageable? Are deadlines realistic? How can I help resolve the recurring issues that are stressing you and causing you to feel overwhelmed? How can I make your work experience better?*

Just keep digging and be persistent. If you have never engaged with your team member on a personal level or shown any interest in their well-being, they will just tell you what you want to hear, and you will be none the wiser. But if you have invested in the relationship early on, they will eventually open up and share their frustrations.

Use your EQ. Practice self-awareness and mind your reaction as information unfolds. Withhold comments and empathize with them. Again, it doesn't mean you have to implicitly agree with their opinion and share their point of view. You just have to recognize their feelings and welcome their input. Later, you can evaluate the merit of their statements, address their concerns, and act.

Similar to Margot's need for structure, your team member may have some simple needs that aren't met. These frustrations gradually pollute the well and lead to disengagement and high turnover.

However, keep in mind that, sometimes, people simply need to vent.

Emotional intelligence is the key that elevates your leadership effectiveness and greatly impacts the culture of your organization. It all flows back to relationships and basic human interactions and you should consider these to be the lifeblood of your business if you want to succeed in the long term.

Much of what happens next—building a collaborative team, delegating, recognizing, coaching, and providing feedback—will be significantly easier if you know your team and have shown them you care. But first, you must set clear expectations for successful outcomes. That's what we'll focus on next.

6
Because I Said So

———

When Jullian turned sixteen and started driving, we bought him a used car. I relished the idea that he'd be driving his younger siblings to and from school, relieving me of my carpool duties.

I had spent the better of the previous eleven years driving up and down I-4, Orlando's main highway. If you're familiar with driving in Central Florida, you'll know that traveling on I-4 feels a lot like extracting yourself from a stopped-up drain, thanks to millions of tourists who flock to the area eager to surrender their paychecks to the local theme parks.

I eventually convinced my husband that we needed to move away from the parks and closer to the kids' school in downtown Orlando. (I'm not sure if *convincing* is the accurate word seeing that I pretty much told him, "The kids and I are moving downtown. Are you joining us?")

So, by the time Jullian turned sixteen, we were living about two miles from the school, which made for a safe and easy commute. However, Dan and I were determined to make this a teaching moment. The keys to freedom for the eager teenager would come at a price.

I mentioned before that we required our children be able to operate the dishwasher and the washing machine before we'd entertain the thought of them operating a car. Dan's wise and pragmatic Uncle Bob and Aunt Cherry also suggested we write down the expectations tied to Jullian getting his own wheels. In doing so, we'd create a contract with our son.

We'd pay for the car and insurance, but Jullian was to earn gas money by doing chores and taking on odd jobs.

We'd cover the cost of maintenance, but it would be Jullian's responsibility to schedule oil changes and regular services.

We expected the car to be kept clean and free of clutter, and always have at *least* a quarter tank of gas. That way, our son wouldn't run low on gas at odd hours and end up having to refuel at a sketchy gas station on the not-so-magical side of town.

And for the first three months, there would be no driving around with friends—I even considered removing all but the driver's seat! There would also be no texting or talking on the phone while driving, and no fidgeting with the radio. We also required him to avoid highways during rush hour as that was the scene of too many accidents and erratic drivers.

For good measure, we added his agreed-upon curfew as a reminder, and we listed all the consequences should he fail to meet any of our requirements.

I admit, all of this would be tough to enforce, but we were serious about making sure Jullian understood our expectations loud and clear, so we typed up the contract, and Jullian, Dan, and I all signed it.

You may think this is overkill, but keep in mind that as a mother, you have two goals in life: To make sure your kids have a better life than you had, and to keep them safe. This took care of the latter.

So Jullian eventually got his hands on the coveted steering wheel. Off he went about town, driving to school and soccer practice. He was always willing to run errands for me, happily jumping at the opportunity to cruise around while blasting his favorite music on the stereo.

The first few months went without a hitch. But like all good things, this eventually came to an end. We started noticing the car looking dirtier and the sticky cups and dirty soccer socks accumulating in the back seat. We had not heard much about oil changes and such, and we suspected a bit of carelessness had generally crept in.

One Sunday night during family dinner, we casually brought up the topic of the car and remarked how neglected it looked. Jullian was quick to assure us of the contrary. "Fair enough, let's check that out after dinner," said my husband.

An hour later, Dan pulled the car into the driveway and proceeded to empty the entire contents of the car *in our front yard*. Well, you would have thought we were having a garage sale! There were tools, books, school papers, enough soccer shirts to equip an entire squad, dirty clothes, hangers, lots of empty soda cans, blankets, pillows, discarded food containers, and a selection of shoes—for the most part unmatched.

I kid you not.

As luck would have it, the gas was also dangerously close to zero, and the service engine light was on. Needless to say, neither Dan nor I were too thrilled, and Jullian was looking pretty sheepish. His siblings were bracing themselves for the storm that was fast approaching. But there was no drama.

I simply pulled up the contract on my laptop, added up the penalties we had stipulated for each transgression, and I let Jullian know how many days he would have to forgo the car and be grounded. This added up to three weeks!

As you well know, teenagers relish their freedom and access to friends, so that was a harsh punishment. However, to our son's credit, he sucked it up and relented. What could have easily turned into an argument, accusations of unfair treatment, or, worse yet, a shouting match and slammed doors went without a squabble. Why? Because the expectations had been clearly stated. There was no room for interpretation.

When things are clear and understood by all parties, there is no need for argument. You go back to what was agreed upon, match it up to the behavior being questioned, and identify the discrepancies and subsequent consequences should any disciplinary actions be required. You highlight what needs to change going forward and then measure progress and improvement.

Jullian took it like a champ. He thoroughly cleaned his car, made an appointment for an oil change, and hopped back into the family carpool for the duration of his punishment.

By the time the three weeks expired, he had a renewed appreciation for independence and autonomy, and he did a much better job at maintaining his car from that point on. Lesson learned!

———

"Because I said so!" How many times have I uttered this sentence? More than I care to remember. Most times, I could rely on the fact that I had set clear expectations. On occasion, I wasn't so sure.

As a leader, you may find yourself in a similar predicament. You may *think* you have been clear on the rules of engagement only to find out that your expectations were not so clear after all.

Yet, setting clear expectations is one of the fundamental responsibilities of leadership. Think about this: What does it mean to lead? On a basic level, most people would agree it is about organizing, directing, and supporting a team to execute a task. Such a task must be well-defined and clearly communicated.

There may be times you know exactly what needs to be done, yet you fail to communicate these goals clearly. In those cases, the lack of successful execution lands squarely on your shoulders.

Your team needs clarity. They need well-defined tasks, precise instructions, and expected outcomes. Here is how to go about it.

Leave No Room for Interpretation

Without clarity, expectations are just noise.

When we told Jullian to keep his car clean, his definition of clean turned out to be a far cry from ours. We learned that when we expected a certain outcome, we needed to provide specific details. So consider what you require in terms of results, behaviors, and communication. **The more time you'll spend thinking through details and bringing clarity ahead of time, the closer you'll get to the desired outcome.**

This will also carry the benefit of making it easier to communicate, allowing you to describe the task well, and assessing if the person assigned feels comfortable with the task.

Do they have questions, doubts, or hesitations? Provide them with an opportunity to express those. Ask questions to make sure they have understood the outcome you are looking for. Better yet, show them.

When I first started working in retail at Disney, I was instructed to demonstrate courtesy—one of the Disney quality standards. I mistakenly thought this meant being courteous by using the "magic words" of *hello*, *please*, *thank you*, and *goodbye*.

"Before you expect someone to do anything for you, understand what it will take to do it well!"
Amalita to Mafalda
Uruapan, Michoacán, Mexico

One day, while I was working at the French Pavilion at Epcot, a leader came to help out in the store. As foot traffic slowed, she took advantage of this lull of activity to ask me about my first two weeks on the job, and we chit-chatted about my adapting to Disney and American culture.

When a guest family entered the store, she greeted them and went on to ask them about their trip, where they were from, and whether they had ever been to France. She kneeled to address the kids at eye level, inquired about their favorite characters, and gave them tips and suggestions for the rest of their time at Disney World. Then she sent them on their way with an enthusiastic, "Have a magical day!"

As I watched the interaction, it became clear to me that the guests' experience at the French Pavilion centered around meeting French citizens and learning a little about French culture along the way. More importantly, the quality of their experience depended on our ability to make them feel special. To me, this leader demonstrated what the interaction should look and feel like. It was Disney's courtesy in action.

Watching her made a lasting impression on me. It painted a vivid picture of the level of service I was supposed to provide. I realized that, up to that point, I hadn't adequately delivered the standards expected of Disney cast members.

It dawned on me that the incident wasn't a coincidence. Even though I had been told what to do, this leader figured out a diplomatic yet efficient way to *demonstrate* the expectations. In doing so, she provided clarity.

I remembered this very lesson when, later in life, I set out to teach my children how to interact with people. I taught them how to shake hands when meeting people and to look them in the eyes when doing so. I expected them to show interest in people by asking questions and making small talk.

While I taught them all these things, I also knew that the best way for them to learn was for me to set an example. Hearing *and* seeing how to do this would give them the clarity needed to imitate what would be expected of them later in life.

Be Realistic

When setting expectations, make sure what you're asking is realistic. Pressured by time and eager to get things done, leaders often fail to think through the assignment.

Ask yourself, *Am I assigning this task to someone who has the ability and the resources to deliver the goods?*

A mother wouldn't put a five-year-old in charge of doing their own laundry. Helping to sort it by colors would be more age appropriate. Later, the mom teaches her child to operate the washing machine, then to fold the clean laundry until, one day, that child can take care of their laundry altogether.

In the same way, tailor your directives to your new team members, and assign the task to the person best equipped to complete it. Team members do not want to appear incompetent and therefore will seldom push back on an assignment—even when they may not have all the skills and resources to take care of it. Remember, they are trying to impress you.

Include a Timeline

In my opinion, the worst acronym in business is without a doubt ASAP. What is "as soon as possible" supposed to mean? To have the task completed in an hour? A day? A week? When time frees up in your calendar?

When asking someone to take care of something ASAP, what you envision might not be within the realm of their possibility. Asking someone to do something ASAP puts unnecessary pressure on the assignee. It implies that completion trumps quality, that this task takes precedence over all other matters.

If this is how you tend to assign deadlines, the joke's on you. Be specific. You want this done by the end of business day? Just say so. Is the assignment due next week? Set a date. Does the project come with a floating deadline? Then set a date regardless but let them know it's negotiable. If you don't want your team member to come to you the night before the due date and ask for an extension, set a deadline for negotiation too.

No matter what, *be specific* regarding timelines and priorities. ASAP is light on details and ineffective to establish an order of priority.

Break Down the Expectations into Specific Behaviors

Your position as a leader gives you a bird's eye view of your organization, your goals, and the resources at your disposal. You also understand which behaviors are needed to ultimately deliver on the expectations.

In Jullian's case, we could have told him, "Be safe!" and hoped for the best. However, we knew it would be much more effective to let him know specifically which behaviors would keep him safe—no phone, no fidgeting with the radio, no friends onboard, and no driving on the highways at rush hour.

The same goes for your team. Being clear on the behavior you expect may seem like overkill, but remember, to be clear is to be kind. If you want them to wear a tie and jacket for your annual awards ceremony, for example, say so and avoid being disappointed at someone's interpretation of *business dress.*

Explain the Why

Having raised three teenagers, I can attest to the fact that they will challenge you and question your every call. I found out that if you explain your reasoning, you have a better chance to have your expectations met.

> *"Because I said so, that's why!"*
> Every Mother to Every Child
> All over the World

Much like teenagers, team members sometimes fail to grasp the impact or long-term implications of an action. Explaining why it is important to you and the team at large will ensure that the odds of compliance are in your favor.

Overcommunicate Expectations

One day, my friend Mary and I went to the movie theater with seven young children. This included our combined five, plus Hannah and Naomi, my friend Marcy's little ones.

The movie was about to start when I passed down a big bag of candy for the kids to share. In the few quiet seconds between the end of a commercial and the beginning of the movie, a small voice rose for everyone to hear. "Miss Valerie, is this candy kosher? Because if it isn't kosher, my mommy says I can't eat it." That was five-year-old Naomi sitting at the very end of the row.

The entire theater laughed out loud. For my part, I could not help but wonder, *How do you communicate expectations so clearly that a five-year-old sitting in the dark without her mother won't eat a piece of candy?*

Repetition. That's how. When expectations are simple and communicated frequently, it stays top of mind. This is how leaders and mothers persuade their team or their children that the behavior they expect from them is *the right thing to do.*

Put It in Writing

Much like we did for Jullian, put your expectations in black and white. This will provide your team with something they can refer to. Some individuals need time to think things through, process their assignments, and clearly understand the expected outcomes. When the time comes to evaluate the quality of your team's work, it will be a lot easier to compare against the expectations you have set.

———

Great leaders are like great moms. Their expectations leave no room for interpretation. They can break down and assign tasks while making sure their team members know what they need to know, have everything they need, and are set up for success. More importantly, they know the reason behind these expectations and can articulate where an assignment connects with their overarching team goals.

Because great leaders always look down the road, they have a clear vision for moving the organization forward. Maybe they hope to acquire additional market shares, improve their brand recognition, venture into a new segment, and make an impact on their industry or their community—even the world.

For a mother, it is ultimately about the kind of life her child will be able to enjoy as an adult, five, ten, twenty years from now. For leaders, it is about setting a long-term target so they can keep growing their business and ensure its sustainability.

7

What Might Be

——————

Dan and I both love sports, and we readily shared this passion with our kids hoping they would eventually pursue a healthy lifestyle and develop a competitive spirit—a hope that did not disappoint.

Margot was a darn good soccer player, a sport she picked up at age seven. I volunteered as a coach for her first year of soccer, and my love for the sport made up for my limited skills. She also played tennis, as I did, and she quickly developed a mean backhand and swift footwork.

I rejoiced in seeing my daughter play the two sports I loved the most, and I was happy to spend time on the sidelines of soccer fields or tennis courts cheering her on.

"Get a career that pays real money, then follow your dreams."
Tami to Susi
Curitiba, Brazil

As her schedule became more packed, Margot chose to forgo tennis so she could dedicate herself entirely to soccer. At eleven, she joined a traveling soccer team. The two of us logged a considerable number of miles as we drove to weekend games throughout Florida and beyond.

Margot stood out on the field with her height, speed, and strength, and she alternatively played outside-back or striker. By the time she turned fourteen, the Orlando City team recruited Margot to play on the Elite Club National League.

Playing in the ECNL involved flying to so-called showcase tournaments around the country, and it resulted in Margot missing many days at school. When we questioned the need for such commitment, coaches were quick to point out Margot's potential, and we entertained the idea of her pursuing soccer at the collegiate level. Margot enjoyed being an athlete and liked the idea.

While I wasn't pinning my hopes on it, I kept an eye down the road thinking of *what could be*. I was determined to help my daughter achieve her potential.

We discussed what being a college athlete implied and what her experience may be. This inspired Margot. She could see the upside of being a college athlete—a wider school choice, the competition, the benefit of having an immediate group of friends, the additional academic tutoring she could get, and possibly even free tuition. She endorsed the idea and started exploring several programs.

I committed to guiding Margot through this process, offering support, advice, and encouragement.

Meanwhile, Jullian and Tristan, great soccer players in their own right, also played competitive soccer on traveling teams, and Dan and I had to make sure the boys could get to their respective matches. This meant that our family of five seldom spent a weekend together. Still, we knew that sacrificing our weekends was a small price to pay to help our kids follow their passion and achieve their dreams.

Everything seemed to head in the right direction for Margot's potential college soccer aspirations. But then came DC.

Georgetown University invited Margot's team to spend time with their Division I soccer team. They took them on a tour of the facilities and practiced some drills with the young girls' team. Next, the team captain and a couple of players held a Q & A session with our girls and shared their daily routine as college athletes.

They mentioned the early morning workout sessions, the twice daily practices, the video reviews, the tutoring to keep up with academic demands, and, of course, the traveling for games. As they spoke, I couldn't help but notice the look on Margot's face. What I read wasn't excitement and interest—instead, she looked overwhelmed and uninspired.

On the ride home, Margot started to reconsider her options. Maybe Division I wasn't such a great idea after all. Could D-III be a better option? It certainly involved less pressure and a more manageable time commitment.

Regardless of her choice, I would support her.

In the months that followed, two of the top D-III colleges showed keen interest in Margot, so she went to visit those schools to meet with the coaching staff. When it came time to commit, she kept dragging her feet. By the fall of her senior year, Margot had finally made up her mind. She did not want to play soccer in college. Period. She wanted to study business and enjoy college life without the implications and requirements of a competitive sport in the mix.

Our plans and long-term vision had come to a screeching halt. Dan and I knew better than to try to change Margot's mind. Her desire to be a college athlete had come and gone.

As mothers, we have big hopes for our kids. We want them to become even more successful than ourselves. We envision great athletic feats, brilliant careers, achievements, and—why not?—acclaims and accolades. With this picture in mind, we attempt to guide them in that direction without over-influencing. We keep reminding ourselves, *It's their lives, their careers, and their dreams—not ours.*

Dan and I had a vivid picture of what Margot's college experience could be, but it was not in the cards. So we went back to square one and helped her recast her net to a broad range of business schools.

What mattered most to us was knowing that she was choosing her own path, even if it meant setting our sights on a totally different horizon. She eventually found her happiness at the University of Colorado Boulder and completed her business degree in marketing while enjoying campus life, multiple internships, and making the most of the beautiful trails and ski runs of Colorado.

> *"Why shouldn't it be you that gets what you want? My money's on you! Make a plan, show some chutzpah, put on a little lipstick, and go for it!"*
> Anette to Aileen
> Virginia Beach, VA, USA

———

Parents should not dictate the long-term goals for their children's lives, but they can certainly help them identify the right path to the career of their choosing. As a leader, you have a bird-eye view of your team, department, or organization. You must provide them with a clear destination, pave the way, and set them on the right path. Though it is tempting and often necessary to keep your head buried in the day-to-day operations of your business, someone needs to keep an eye down the road and chart a course of action. *What are we trying to achieve? Where do we want to go?* These are existential questions for which you, as a leader, must provide an answer.

As you set the foundation for a successful enterprise, you need to define what success will look like and then build your strategy around that vision. Sounds simple, doesn't it?

It would amaze you to see how many leaders "in name only" neither identify a clear objective nor establish a comprehensive strategy. Some of them succeed in spite of themselves, but that success is often short-lived. Without a clear vision, team members can get easily confused, side-tracked, discouraged, or frustrated.

To ensure you muster the commitment and enthusiasm of your team, here are some milestones you must pay attention to.

Have a Clear Destination

Defining a clear organizational vision starts with you as the leader. You must know where you want to take your team, your project, your department, or—if you're the ultimate decision maker—your company.

This vision becomes your North Star, the destination that anchors your strategy and determines the playbook by which your entire team must operate. It allows you to stay focused on the most important aspects of your business.

Start by figuring out where you hope to be in five or ten years. Think about it thoroughly and fill in all the blanks. The more detailed a plan you can provide, the easier you and your team can stay on course.

Your vision shouldn't be a financial goal. Financial goals are uninspiring. Moms do not wake up their kids in the morning by telling them they need to go to school to get good grades. They bait them with the learning, the socializing, and the fun that awaits.

Paint a picture that will captivate your team's imagination, something that will get you and your team out of bed knowing you are collectively working toward a great destination. No one wants to follow a leader when the target is marred with indecision and hesitation. Employees engage when the objectives are clear, they can see the path, and the overall goals are striking.

To open up further possibilities, enlist the help of close collaborators, even outside partners—anyone who can bring innovation, foresight, and a pioneering spirit to the table. The perspective of outsiders brings a new way of thinking and may expand the horizon.

Be Ambitious yet Realistic

Your vision must be aspirational yet rooted in the strengths, talents, and uniqueness of your organization. You would not steer your children toward a career they have no skills or aptitude for. Likewise, you should not lead your team or company down a path if you are lacking the will, the means, or the resources for the task. So make sure your vision aligns with what you have at your disposal.

If you are lacking any of the above and feel strongly that it is the right long-term goal, focus your energy on filling these gaps before you move forward. Nothing kills enthusiasm faster than aiming for an unattainable destination.

Share Your Vision

Ambitious organizational goals cannot become reality without the work and commitment of an entire team. Steer the imagination of your team members and turn passive contributors into active participants.

Your team can only see so far. As a result, they restrict their ambitions to their immediate environment. Enlarge their vision by painting a picture of *all that could be.*

Think about it: When mothers ask their children what they want to be when they grow up, most young kids will respond that they want to be a teacher, a doctor, a firefighter, or an athlete. They might even gravitate toward the profession of their parents. Why? It's *what they know.* So mothers take it upon themselves to open their children's eyes to the myriad of possibilities that life offers.

That's also what leaders can do for their teams: expand their horizons and let them see what may be. Help them envision how they can be part of that future and take ownership of the initiative, understanding how their roles and responsibilities may contribute to the big picture.

> "You can be whatever you want to be."
> Sunshine to Cherry
> Chevy Chase, MD, USA

Most people work for money and benefits. But **they also want to be relevant and contribute to something greater than the sum of their responsibilities**.

Younger generations entering the workforce today are mindful of the footprint they will leave behind and how they impact the world around them. They aspire to be part of a greater goal *and* a greater good. And it is up to you as the leader to provide that, to cast a vision worth pursuing.

Personal growth is also a prime motivation. Most employees look for upward mobility in an organization. If yours isn't a company where they can see the direction you're moving in, the best employees will quickly get bored and look for a more promising future somewhere else.

Great team members aspire to develop, stretch their skills, expand their knowledge, and tackle new and inspiring projects. A company that has no clear long-term objectives and strategy offers none of the above.

Keep It Front and Center

Once you've set your mind on a destination, your vision needs to permeate your entire organization—from decision-making to recognition and feedback. It should become the yardstick by which you measure progress.

Disney does this exceptionally well. The company's sole goal is to create magical experiences for its guests and, in doing so, to become the number-one entertainment company. As a result, "making magic" is part of every bit of internal communication, recognition, performance feedback, and storytelling that takes place every day across all Disney theme parks and hotels.

Whether cast members work directly with guests or in a support role, whether they are hourly employees or executives, everyone has their eyes on the goal. And boy, do they deliver! It may feel like Pixie Dust overkill, but it works.

You can ask any cast member, "What are we doing today?" and they'll tell you they're making magic. Let me tell you, when you make something the centerpiece of everything you talk about and do, it becomes muscle memory.

How do you make this happen? You must communicate, communicate, communicate. Isn't repetition a mother's favorite form of pedagogy? Think how often mothers remind their kids to brush their teeth until it becomes part of their daily routine. Similarly, if you want to rally your team around a goal, it will take repetition. You can't just stick a vision statement on a wall or your website and dust it off once a year.

Once a vision is fully ingrained in the DNA of an organization, building a strategy becomes easier. You can start with your target in mind and weigh every decision you make against it, aim all your expectations toward that destination, and ensure that each step goes in that direction.

Be Prepared to Change

If you notice the competition biting at your heels, you're struggling to make strides, have trouble attracting applicants to job openings, or you're dealing with attrition, it may be time to reassess your long-term goals. Maybe your vision is not keeping pace with reality. Maybe it is outdated and has gotten stale. Maybe it fails to inspire.

Things change, and they change fast. Remember that the path to success isn't as clear-cut as it used to be. It is now blurred by the constant advances in technology and by globalization.

The workplace and the market now require new skills. Consider your team as if it were your child. As your team members grow and mature, you get a better understanding of their uniqueness, strengths, and potential. Sometimes this potential isn't enough to deliver the vision you had hoped for. Sometimes the competition in your field has become too intense. If you can't address these issues, don't hesitate to tweak or reframe your vision, or even change direction entirely. Some leaders and organizations who have failed to do this paid the price in the long term.

Much like with Margot's soccer career, you sometimes must be prepared to fold and draw a new hand. That is not only perfectly OK; it is necessary for today's environment. As the saying goes, **you can't direct the wind, but you can adjust the sails.**

———

With raising kids, mothers provide their children with a springboard, not a fast track. A fast track can cause tunnel vision, short-sightedness, blind spots—even a dead end. On the other hand, the springboard gives kids momentum, propels them upward, and more importantly provides them with a broader perspective. As a leader, you must think of that vision as being the springboard for your business.

> *"Trust your instinct and move forward!"*
> Dany to Veronique
> Santeny, France

———

So you've set the stage for success. You've made sure you hired partners and team members for whom character matters. You've created effective onboarding and training processes, and you've not only built rapport, but you continue to nurture healthy relationships. You've set clear expectations and you've cast a clear vision to guide your team and your organization toward an ambitious goal. The foundational elements are now in place.

Next, you can focus your attention on the day-to-day behaviors that will fuel employee engagement. These are what I call the **modus operandi of leadership**: creating an environment of trust, providing feedback, rewarding teams, communicating effectively, and modeling the appropriate behaviors . . . things that leaders must focus on every day.

These leadership habits convert employees into productive and highly engaged team members. That's what we'll focus on in Part 2.

PART 2

———

Modus Operandi

8
Trust in Me

———

Our youngest son, Tristan, has always been fearless. While Jullian and Margot were active and adventurous, he was an absolute daredevil. By the time he was just six months old, Tristan could escape from his crib.

By the time he could crawl, he'd hidden in our kitchen cabinets, climbed onto the bathroom counters, and even got into the dryer when I turned my back. Once, Tristan grabbed onto the garage door while it was opening and hung on as it rose so he could dangle from the ceiling! And he did all this before he turned two.

By the time Tristan was six, we knew to look *up* whenever he'd disappear. We'd find him at the very top of a tree, on the roof of the house, or on the top rung of a ladder. At age ten, he took up Parkour, a sport that involves running and jumping over urban obstacles while doing flips and somersaults.

Well-meaning mothers would lecture me about how irresponsible I was for allowing Tristan to do what he did, but I knew my son's innate athletic abilities, and I trusted that he instinctively knew what he could and could not do—even though I was terrified at times. I'm pleased to report that he reached adulthood unscathed, for the most part, at least.

The fact is, one of the hardest responsibilities of motherhood is to keep children safe while raising them to operate independently and step out on their own at the appropriate time.

Having the instinct to protect those we love—especially those we raised—letting go seems counterintuitive. But mothers also understand that if kids are to grow up into independent human beings, there comes a time when they need to step back and let their children try things for themselves, make their own decisions, and take risks. Even though our maternal instinct propels us to protect them, we know we shouldn't shield them from challenges or failures.

So, early on, we loosen our grip and gradually allow our children some leeway. At home, we let toddlers select their outfits, turning a blind eye to fashion faux pas. We let them decide what foods they like or not, and on the playground, we let our kids put their physical abilities to the test and choose their playmates.

During these early years, we let our kids gradually assert themselves and gain confidence in their own decision-making abilities. Ultimately, they learn to trust their own judgment knowing full well that mom is there for support and counsel, if need be.

Once a child reaches middle school, they're more strongly influenced by their friends and, regrettably, TV and social media. So the dynamic changes. While our children can still rely on us for all physiological needs, they start to challenge our judgment.

By the time they are full-fledged teenagers, they pull away and isolate. This presents a significant trust hurdle. During this time, kids seek more privacy, but mothers tend to imagine the worst. (Let me tell you, the possibilities are endless.)

Mothers try to navigate these treacherous waters with diplomacy, patience, and self-control—some days successfully, some days . . . not so much. There's often much eye-rolling involved. As teens lobby for more freedom, mothers must determine how much to trust their judgment.

During this time, we aim to strike the right balance between being too permissive or overbearing. There's no magic formula. The degree to which we trust their judgment depends on how well we know our child. That is why we try to keep an open line of communication at all times and engage in discussing sometimes mundane topics, hoping to glean relevant information. We gently probe our teenagers with questions trying to assess their mindset or identify issues they may be dealing with.

Teenagers are like oysters—they eventually open up. And any mother knows to listen attentively when that happens so they may learn about the challenges their children face, the decisions they make, the individuals they look up to, and the friends they surround themselves with. Slowly and subtly, mothers try to impart some words of wisdom or gentle advice, hoping that they can influence their teenagers.

During these conversations, there are pearls of information to be harvested so that mutual understanding eventually forms and eases some of the natural maternal anxiety.

Throughout their childhood, there will be occasional breaches of trust—sometimes just a simple fib as children try to wiggle their way out of trouble. We once caught eight-year-old Jullian red-handed.

> *"Tell me who you hang out with, and I'll tell you who you are."*
> Ms. Luci to Vanessa
> Itajubá, Minas Gerais, Brazil

He had forgotten to get our approval for a field trip and had attempted to forge a signature on the release form so he could submit it on time. Realizing what a poor counterfeiter he was, he had hilariously written "In a hurry" next to the signature, hoping to escape suspicion. We had a big talk about trust and, you guessed it, we grounded Jullian, and he did not attend the field trip.

Other times, a breach of trust can be more consequential. We once got an alarming late-night phone call from Tristan when he was seventeen. "I am with the police," he told us. "You have to come pick me up."

Well, I mentioned earlier that Tristan loves Parkour and jumps at every opportunity (no pun intended) to test his skills. That evening, he and two of his friends entered a construction site where they had noticed a sandpile right underneath what was to become a two-story parking garage. It was the perfect landing pad for a somersault.

The construction site was not fenced in, but it was private property nonetheless, so the boys were trespassing. Someone noticed them and called the cops.

The police officers, who no doubt had bigger fish to fry, were keen to teach these teenagers a lesson. After initially scaring the boys out of their wits by threatening to press charges, the officers offered to let the boys go on one condition: They had to ask their parents to come and pick them up at the construction site.

When we arrived, the officers reassured us by discreetly telling us that the boys had immediately complied with them and had been very respectful throughout the encounter.

We thanked the officers, drove home in silence, and sent Tristan to his room, postponing the confrontation until the next morning. We had to allow time for our anger to dissipate knowing full well that emotionally charged situations are not conducive to teaching moments.

The next morning, we calmly discussed with Tristan the implications of his poor judgment. First, he had failed to stick to what was initially agreed upon (going out for a burger with his friends). Second, he and his friends had illegally entered a site, and that could have had dramatic consequences.

Considering Florida being a "stand your ground" state, it would have been within the rights of a security guard on the property to shoot them on the spot. In the dark, someone could have easily confused three teenagers with unscrupulous robbers. None of that had crossed the boys' minds.

As mothers understand all too well, teenagers rarely think through the consequences of their decisions. Tristan and his friends had made a mistake. There was no break-in, no damage done, and they never entered that site with criminal intent. Regardless, we grounded Tristan, and he lost his driving and outing privileges until he could show better judgment. His poor decision did not warrant the level of freedom we had granted him, and he would have to earn back our trust.

> *"Always look further than the tip of your nose."*
> Anna to Annick
> Lyon, France

Dan and I told him we were very disappointed with his poor judgment and hoped he would learn from this and bounce back. And that, he did.

Looking back, we recognized how lucky we were. While this could have taken a dramatic turn, it turned out to be the perfect teaching moment, one about honesty, the consequences of our actions, and the importance of trust.

———

If motherhood has taught me anything, it is that trust can fuel relationships with our children, as it does with our spouse and with our friends. I discovered it is also the nucleus of great team-work and is a prerequisite to any sustainable enterprise.

A couple of years ago, I was consulting for a company where the top salesperson was notorious for being ruthless in business. He was a selfish loner who often displayed contempt for the rest of the team and for the organization's values and code of conduct. His was the not-so-uncommon mentality that *the end justifies the means.*

No one trusted him. As a result, the morale of the team suffered. My recommendation was to document all the incidents in order to terminate the individual. But the leader of the organization didn't seem too thrilled with my advice. He lamented, "How can I? He's my number-one sales guy. He delivers results!"

I explained how this individual impacted the company's culture. He polluted the environment for everyone else. Besides, he was setting a poor example that someone was bound to emulate. Things would deteriorate if they had not already.

Turning a blind eye to such behavior is like failing to fix a broken window. Water will gradually work its way in, and it won't be long until humidity turns to mold. The same goes for an organization. If you don't fix this kind of behavior right away, it quickly becomes contagious.

Several months later, the leader had finally had enough, and he fired the guy. When I asked him if his business had suffered as a result, he reluctantly admitted, "No. In fact, sales are better than ever before!"

Turns out that everyone else's productivity had improved, and this largely made up for losing their number-one sales guy. Why? Because the unscrupulous individual was so unreliable and dishonest, the other team members had been wasting time watching their backs and second-guessing everything. Morale was low and turnover high.

With him gone, everyone focused again on doing their job in the best way possible. Trust was restored and the entire team collaborated willingly. With that, morale and results improved.

I'm sharing this story to highlight the direct link between trust and productivity. Much like families, organizations cannot operate effectively without trust. Trust affects the well-being of everyone involved and ultimately affects the bottom line. This is why leaders must make every effort to create an environment of trust. Here's how you can start.

Build Strong Relationships

If I haven't made it abundantly clear in Chapter 4, be intentional about spending time with your team members. Facilitate conversations where work is off the table. Pay attention to what is being said during these interactions, even if seemingly insignificant. It may seem insignificant to you, but not to them. They may test you and, much like a teenager would, they may assess how much to share.

Think about this: When you first meet someone, you don't know if they're competent, honest, reliable, smart, filled with good intentions, etc. This gap in knowledge makes you uneasy.

You trust people when you have shared experiences that provide you with an understanding of their abilities, their style, their strengths and weaknesses, and their reliability. You can then calibrate your expectations accordingly. (Granted, your history with them can also be a reason not to trust them.)

Relationships form the genesis of trust. Where there is trust, there is great communication. Where there is great communication, there is no second-guessing each other, and effective delegation comes easy. And when delegated to, team members feel empowered. Where there is empowerment, there is ownership.

Where there is ownership, there is motivation. Where there is motivation, there is creativity and risk-taking and problem-solving and resilience and, ultimately, success.

Forging great relationships feeds this cycle and has the most substantial impact on your ability to trust each other.

Facilitate Informal Team Gatherings

If they don't already, encourage team members to build strong relationships within the group. There is something to be said about a fifteen-minute coffee break. This is when your team can relax and bond. With time, this generates greater cooperation between your team members.

If you lead remote teams, you can do the same through scheduled virtual coffee breaks or happy hour. These can come with automated alerts to invite team members to join in. Some organizations put in place a daily study-hall format where team members log in and work alongside each other virtually for a couple of hours. They can casually interact while working independently.

Unstructured interactions are often a substantial source of valuable information. As a mom, I found my kids and I had the best conversations in the car to and from school. Carpool time offered an unguarded moment when they were more inclined to talk, not only to me but also among siblings and friends. During those times, they'd forget I was there, and I'd simply listen.

So be purposeful and persistent about facilitating casual conversations with and among your team. It will pay off sooner than later.

Be Trustworthy

No matter the quality of the relationship, trust isn't a given. You have to *earn* it. And the surest way to become a trusted leader is to *be trustworthy*.

How do you do that? First, remember that all eyes are on you. So do what you say you'll do. Live your values. Show up when you say you will. Practice transparency and explain the reason behind your decisions. Be consistent and fair. Remember what teammates shared with you. Keep confidential information to yourself. Don't deflect and deny. Be honest and tell the truth. In other words, set an example that team members can emulate.

> "Live a life that will make your ancestors proud."
> Sachiko-san to Etsuko-san
> Ishinomaki, Miyagi, Japan

Going back to a mother's playbook: When mothers want to earn their teenagers' trust, they know they must be reliable and fair, accessible yet not overbearing. They must provide answers without lecturing. They must respect their teenagers' privacy and know when to engage. They must keep their promises and be there when their teen needs them. And they must be consistent in their decisions and judgment.

Practice Accountability

You may be full of good intentions, but you're also human. There will be times when you make a mistake. When you do, accept responsibility, and apologize. It shows humility and vulnerability. Gone are the days when leaders were expected to know it all and do everything right. Admitting when you've made mistakes makes you more relatable.

And when your team sees you owning your mistakes, they are less likely to fear making mistakes themselves. As the saying goes: Better to trust the man who is frequently in error than the one who is never in doubt. Besides, nothing like a seemingly perfect boss to squash initiatives and risk-taking!

Be Respectful of Everyone

And I mean *everyone*. Even if they're not in the room with you, show respect. If you make judgmental comments about others in their absence—even if it's someone in a different department or company—those in the room with you will wonder, *What would this person say about me if I weren't here?* There is no surer way to erode trust.

Share the Spotlight

Be quick to recognize others' contributions and give credit where credit is due. It shows fairness, honesty, and integrity. All three are ethical behaviors that will earn you the respect of others and move the needle toward mutual trust.

Trust Others

It warrants repeating: You have to be worthy of your team's trust. And if you want to earn it, you may have to take a leap of faith and start extending trust to your collaborators and team members.

Some leaders are reluctant to hand over responsibilities and decision-making for fear of mistakes and their consequences.

Admittedly, mothers feel the same way. It takes willpower to entrust young children with some of the household chores. Assigning them to do the laundry, for example, is fraught with the risk of ending up with a collection of tie-dye shirts. Sometimes, it can be tempting (and faster) to just do the work ourselves. However, mothers understand that if they hope to delegate tasks to their kids in the long run, inevitably it requires placing trust in their children's abilities even if it is at the expense of a perfect outcome.

The same is true in the workplace. You may be afraid that mistakes reflect poorly on your reputation and leadership ability.

So, what do you do? You check and double-check, micromanage, look over everyone's shoulders, cover up mistakes, and become an overbearing leader akin to a helicopter mom. You compromise trust, the team disengages, and performance suffers. Listen, you cannot afford to be *that* leader. Get over it!

Think about everything you could be doing if you trusted others. The more tasks you delegate, the more time you free up. You can then focus on more strategic issues and prepare for long-term projects.

By the way, the upside to transferring authority to your team step by step is that they can develop the skills required to—you guessed it—take on greater responsibilities. You are now feeding the cycle: trust, delegate, develop, and repeat. Do this until your team members are ready for a step up and a promotion.

Delegating requires that you trust their abilities and judgment little by little. Assign them more important tasks over time and work your way up gradually—even if it costs you a few mistakes along the way. Your team will reward you with their trust and with better performance.

As Lao-Tzu says, "He who does not trust cannot be trusted."

> "You don't make an omelet without breaking a few eggs."
> Anna to Annick
> Lyon, France

———

What if none of this works? What if you have modeled all the right behaviors yet come up empty-handed? It may be that something in your teammate's history—their experiences with you or with others and the beliefs those have sprouted—is keeping them from extending trust. That is why **you cannot *build* trust.**

What do I mean by that? Trust takes time to grow. You simply cannot force someone to trust you. Only *they* can decide. You can only control your behavior, not theirs. Give it time and stay the course. But don't beat yourself up if you cannot make headway.

What to Do When There's a Breach of Trust

When trust has been breached—and it will happen—do not ignore it. Deal with it. Allow for emotions to settle, then ask yourself if you can recover from this experience. Sometimes you know deep inside that no matter what unfolds, there is no going back.

Years ago at Disney, I became suspicious of dwindling sales and missing inventory in my store. A bit of investigating revealed that one of the newly promoted supervisors was not only helping himself to cash from the register, but he was also stealing inventory that he was reselling out of the trunk of his car.

I suspected several cast members were aware of what was going on—if not willing participants. Along with some security cast members, I privately questioned every employee, and several of them spilled the beans.

It turned out that all but two of my employees were implicated in the scam. Some admitted to stealing, others were mere spectators but never reported it for fear of retribution from their supervisor.

This left me with a decision: Should I just fire the active participants but keep the passive onlookers? After all, most of them were young and in their first job ever. It was easy for the supervisor to manipulate them. I dreaded firing almost an entire crew during our busy season. Doing so would cause all kinds of headaches until I could fill the open positions again.

I mulled this over, but not for very long. I ended up firing everyone involved in the scam, including those passive spectators.

I realized I could not work with a team I couldn't fully trust. I was convinced that I'd have to keep looking over their shoulders to ensure the same didn't happen again.

Trust had been broken, and I couldn't see a way to mend fences.

In retrospect, I realize this was not a hard decision; the issue was an ethical one. But most trust issues are not that clear-cut.

Regardless of the issue at stake, it's important to think about the long-term implications of the breach: *Will we be able to move on? Will we be able to collaborate and partner in the future?* Then you can decide if the relationship is sustainable and worthwhile.

To determine whether trust can be restored or not, consider the circumstances. Ask yourself, *Did I fail to see the writing on the wall? Were there signs that I may be trusting this person too quickly? Does this breach of trust reflect the character of the individual?*

Thinking back on the circumstances of Tristan's late-night encounter with the police, I could honestly answer a resounding *no* to all the above.

Going through this exercise can help you gain perspective and prevent you from jumping to conclusions or envisioning the worst. You may realize that the event was unintentional and a genuine mistake.

Then, decide how to address the issue.

You may be tempted to opt for a radical solution, the business version of "You're grounded . . . for life!" Or you may be tempted to simply carry on, determined to never trust the individual again. I don't know about you but living or working in an environment fraught with distrust isn't something I'm willing to do.

Neither of these options will make you feel any better, nor will they bring you any closer to a solution. Resentment will set in and fester. So buckle up and address the issue with the perpetrator. Here's how.

Have an honest conversation. Explain why you feel betrayed or disappointed. Let the offender know that trust has eroded. Listen to what that person has to say. Then ask yourself, *Does the individual show genuine concern? Do they understand why I am feeling the way I do? Is this person willing to change their behavior?*

> "The most important thing in life is to always be honest."
> Cilmara to Annie Marie
> Balneário Camboriú, Brazil

Again, thinking of Tristan's case, when presented with these questions, it was clear that he understood our reaction, and he was genuinely sorry for his lapse in judgment. It allowed us to move on to the next step and find a new way forward.

However, if you sense the person doesn't understand your rationale, shows no remorse, or is unwilling to change, it's a non-starter. It might be a sign that this breach of trust isn't the result of circumstances, but of poor character. This may be irreversible, and trust is beyond repair. It's time to send your "number-one sales guy" to find his happiness somewhere else!

Move from finger-wagging to problem-solving. Again, ask yourself: *How will this work going forward? Are there new rules I can put in place so we can trust each other once again?*

Both parties must understand that regaining trust is a long process, and there's no guarantee that you can totally mend it. However, clearing the air and laying down the foundation for a fresh start will improve the odds. You'll need a new process, additional checkpoints, and enhanced and more frequent communication.

As for Tristan, he gradually regained his privileges. He completed his punishment without a peep, became 100% reliable with all his chores, and took care of assignments without complaining.

Meanwhile, I encouraged him along the way to show him he was making progress.

As we reinstated his privileges one by one, Tristan followed the new ground rules with zeal, communicated with us diligently, and regained our unconditional trust. It's fair to add that he'll probably never again enter a construction site without permission. When you experience broken trust, it may cause you to question whether things will ever get back to normal. Ironically, I have found that if you deal with the issue head-on, clear the air, and work toward a resolution, you may find that you come out on the other end with a stronger relationship and possibly an even stronger level of trust than you thought possible.

———

As challenging as it may be to create an environment of trust, I have found that it has an invaluable return on investment: **Mutual trust puts leaders in a much better position to fuel team performance with effective recognition and constructive feedback.**

Why is that? Employees know that you have their backs and best interests at heart. They will look upon your positive *and* negative remarks favorably and welcome your input, whether you're recognizing them for a job well done or coaching them for improvement.

As you'll see in the chapters that follow, I will continue to draw from mothers' playbooks. After all, their innate expertise in the fields of recognition and feedback is undeniable and, I would argue, unmatched.

9
Dispensing Tough Love

———

When I graduated from high school, I had my sights set on a career that would involve a fair amount of traveling. I wasn't sure what job that would be, but I had a burning curiosity to go see the world.

I knew speaking English would open many doors, so I parlayed my way into a gap year and moved to North London to work as an au pair. Eighteen months later, I returned to France with a newfound mastery of the Queen's English, moved back in with my parents, and started my undergraduate studies.

My experience in London had been gratifying in more ways than one. I particularly relished the freedom to lead my life unburdened by parental supervision. As I resumed student life in France, I carried on with the same independence and went about my social life with little thought for my new living arrangements, that is, being back under my parents' roof.

One night, some friends suggested an impromptu dinner gathering. I happily obliged.

When I got home later that night, the house was dark and the front door bolted from the inside. I assumed my parents had mistakenly locked me out.

When I knocked, the lights turned on immediately, and my mom opened the door. Before I could apologize, she asked, "Where were you?"

I casually answered, "Just out with some friends."

"We were expecting you for dinner and waited for you to show up," my mom continued. "We were worried about you!" Keep in mind, this was long before cell phones had become an extension of our limbs, and I had not taken the time to call home to let my parents know I would not be home for dinner.

"If you can party, you can work!"
Helga to Christine
Bad Salzuflen, Germany

Before I could think it through, I retorted, "Mom, when I lived in London, you had no idea where I was! You didn't worry then. Why is this any different?"

My mom seemed to consider my response for a minute and then quietly stated, "Well, that's no problem. However, if you treat this house as a hotel and show up as you wish without warning or notice, we will start charging you the rate of a hotel." Mic drop.

I was dumbfounded. I had felt so righteous that I had not realized that my mother had cooked a meal for me, had set the table, had delayed dinner time expecting me to come home, had agonized about all the things that may have happened to me when I didn't show up, and had finally settled on the couch anxiously awaiting my return.

By the time I recovered my senses, my mom had gone to bed, leaving me to mull over the lesson. It has been thirty-five years, and I still vividly remember that night!

When there is a need for feedback, no one delivers more effectively than a mom. In fact, if feedback were an Olympic discipline, I guarantee mothers would be the Dream Team and beat everyone hands down. Moms are always ready to tell you what's what in no uncertain terms.

I bet your mom's litany of directives and recommendations still echoes in your head: "You forgot to wash your hands." "This outfit isn't appropriate. You need to go change." "Be nice and share with others." "Don't chew with your mouth open." "Slow down. You're going too fast." "Plan ahead." "Stop this, right now!" It may have sounded and felt like nagging, but those directives came with good intent.

No matter how much I resented my mom's feedback when I was growing up, once I became a mom, I understood where it stemmed from. A mother's feedback is not *devoid* of love, it is *because* of love. Mothers want the best for their children. They have big plans for them and understand their kids' future is contingent on their ability to become well-rounded adults. So they will let their children know in no uncertain terms when their behavior is inappropriate or unacceptable.

Because we love our children unconditionally, **our motivation isn't to judge or condemn; it is about changing a behavior.**

And in correcting a child, we do so promptly. We don't wait for a year-end review to say, "You behaved badly this year. Here's what you did."

We know bad behavior will be harder to change if left unchecked. So we **provide coaching EVERY SINGLE DAY.** We observe behaviors and correct them as we go.

Keyword: *observe.* We see everything. Moms use their legendary "eyes in the back of the head" to keep track of their brood. If we do not have a clear visual of the situation, we know not to rely on hearsay. We wait to get the facts. But rest assured, when we suspect mischief, we focus our attention on YOU!

Raising kids is a tough assignment that's often met with little to no gratitude . . . until years later, when our children become adults. That's when they realize what we have been doing all along—setting them up for a happy and fulfilling life as a well-rounded, well-mannered, respectful adult. And just like that, one random day, our children might let us know how much they appreciate what we have taught them. That day, we kick up our heels, order a really nice cocktail with a paper umbrella, and give ourselves a great big pat on the back. We can bask in the moment, knowing that we fully deserve it!

I know, I know. We don't always get it right. Show me a mother who has never uttered words she wishes she could take back, and I'll show you a flying hippo.

Do mothers ever say things they regret, be it out of exasperation, an emotional outburst, or simply a poor choice of words? You bet. When a situation is emotionally charged, things can get out of hand. In those moments, even though the heart and head know better, the mouth just won't stop.

Correcting behavior requires finesse, diplomacy, the right tone, and the appropriate words. But amid the daily mayhem, it can be hard for a mom to think straight.

"I am busier than a one-armed wallpaper hanger."
Ella to Dink
Ardmore, OK, USA

Even though it is always best to wait for things to cool down, we sometimes just do not have that luxury. Some matters are just too pressing; we must address them right away.

This is why it is important to make a distinction between the different kinds of feedback. There is the everyday, run-of-the-mill feedback that addresses small matters. I consider these behavioral adjustments, or Behavior 101. This kind of feedback doesn't require long explanations or justification. They're straightforward directives that are dispensed on the go.

"Because you wait till the last minute to get ready, it causes the entire family to be late."

"Leave your brother alone. He needs to concentrate so he can finish his homework."

"If you refuse to share your toys, this play date is over, and we are going home."

At least, that's what we *mean* to say. We don't always have the time, patience, or discipline to explain the why behind our remarks, even if we can rationalize every single one of them. So what comes out of our mouths often sounds more like (cue the exasperated tone),

"Hurry, we're late!"

"Leave him alone!"

"Be nice!"

In Behavior 101, we only address trivial matters. However, issues of consequence require more pointed conversations. That's Behavior 201. As kids grow up, we deliver less of the former and increasingly more of the latter.

Mothers certainly don't give feedback to a five-year-old the same way they do to a fifteen-year-old. During the teenage years, moms must teach more subtle behaviors. Those include being attentive to others and their feelings, developing polished social skills, reading a room, and self-regulating your reactions.

Teenagers are not always receptive to feedback—quite an understatement—and moms understand they are past the point of *telling them what to do.* It is a matter of *influencing them* instead.

So mothers use a more careful approach and abide by some simple rules of engagement: They look for the right time and place when the feedback is more likely to land well, they never dispense feedback in public, they explain the why, and they watch how their teen responds.

Do mothers get pushback? Of course. Do teenagers deflect and deny responsibility? Absolutely. Hence, another important rule: Moms make sure they collect all the facts before they have "the talk," and they come ready to explain their rationale.

Mothers also come prepared with practical advice. Teenagers need guidance on how to improve and the confidence that they can turn things around. They also need to know that mistakes are as much part of growing up as growth spurts and growing pains are.

Mothers don't expect perfection. They understand that failure is a good thing and that adversity forges character. They deliver feedback, then step back to let their teens internalize the lessons and change their behavior.

> "Just do your best. That's all I can ask for."
> Sue to Megs
> Cape Town, South Africa

Eventually, the feedback dispensed over the years pays off, and teenagers might come to appreciate the value of their mom's guidance. They continue to engage and ask for advice—even into adulthood. They will sometimes rely on their mom to help them overcome blind spots and delicate situations. This would be Behavior 301. It is like upskilling, a subtle way to help a grown child become the best person they can be.

No matter the circumstances, giving feedback may not yield the results mothers seek right away. If there is one thing they know for sure, it's that persistence powers persuasion and ultimately changes behaviors.

———

In all the responsibilities of a leader, giving feedback is the one thing we most often shy away from. There are several reasons we dread giving feedback: We don't know how, we're afraid of the reaction, we don't have all the facts, we're uncomfortable, or maybe we care too much and are afraid of hurting the other person's feelings. Sometimes we aren't even sure we've correctly set the expectations. (If that is indeed the reason, I refer you back to Chapter 6).

You can circumvent many of these reasons by drawing from a mother's playbook. These few rules of thumb will help the medicine go down.

Keep It Private

No one wants to be coached in front of an audience—not a child, not a teenager, and certainly not a professional. As a young leader, I found myself in hot water. Out of expediency, I had let some comments slip at an inopportune time. Not only did the feedback land with a thud, but I lost credibility as a leader. So count to ten before blabbering something untimely and regretful.

Make Sure You've Observed the Behavior Firsthand

Consider the behavior you're aiming to correct. Have you observed it in person? If not, let it go. Mothers know not to rely on a sibling's tattle tale. The same goes for the workplace. Only provide feedback on behaviors you know to be true rather than based on office gossip. You need a thorough understanding of the circumstances to avoid making assumptions or jumping to conclusions based on hearsay. This way, you can see it as serving "truth back," not giving feedback.

Deliver Feedback in Person

Speaking face-to-face adds tone, intent, and body language to the delivery and leaves no room for interpretation. Besides, you want to assess the person's reaction in real time. Is it irrational, or is it controlled? Do they take responsibility for their actions or deny and deflect? Are they defensive? Also, pay attention to the person's body language. Delivering feedback in person will provide you with all you need to know about their willingness to improve.

Make It Timely

Deliver feedback while it is top of mind for everyone involved. The longer you wait, the harder it gets and the fuzzier the facts. It is tempting to punt the ball downfield and postpone a tough conversation, hoping it becomes a non-issue or rationalizing that you'll address it the next time it happens. Don't wait. Do it. And do it *now*!

Unacceptable behaviors quickly become contagious. Not only will others pick up on the poor example, but you will slowly and surely lose credibility as a leader.

While working at Disney, it didn't take long for me to learn that cast members would ignore appearance guidelines if I wasn't vigilant and diligent about correcting even minor violations right away.

So I developed a hawk's eye for missing nametags, oversized jewelry, shaggy haircuts, and wild manicures. If one person could get away with breaking the rules, others would follow. And if I would wait to address someone down the line, the culprit would question me for letting others get away with it. How would I justify coaching the second, third, or fourth offender rather than the first?

If you're tempted to put off giving feedback, ask yourself: *What am I afraid of? That the person may quit?* Then remind yourself of the alternative: *What if I don't correct the behavior and they stay?* That should provide all the motivation you need to soldier on.

Review Expectations

When providing feedback, consider the behavior that is under scrutiny. Is the issue clear-cut? If so, think along the lines of Behavior 101: This is the problem, and this is the solution. These instances are straightforward and often relate to technical skills.

So don't beat around the bush. Simply state the facts and nothing but the facts. Let the team member know exactly what you expect going forward. End the conversation with a word of encouragement so they know you have confidence in their ability to turn things around. Short and sweet.

If the issue is more subjective and includes some gray areas or some sensitive matters, be especially mindful of how you present it. Shoot for Behavior 201. Give the team member the opportunity to identify the mistake on their own. For example, state what you noticed:

> *"Don't waste your time with regret. Get up, learn your lesson, stand tall, and keep walking."*
> Maria Carlota to Reina
> Montevideo, Uruguay

"It seems you were unprepared for this meeting. Would you agree?"

"You appear reluctant to work and communicate with your peers during the rollout of this new initiative. Anything I should know about?"

A great follow-up question may be: "If you could go back in time, would you handle this differently?" Your team member's answer will let you know if they are genuinely interested in changing behavior. If they cannot submit a solution that meets your standards, you may want to refer them back to the expectations you have laid out for your team.

Provide Constructive Feedback

After giving the team member an opportunity to respond, highlight the impact of their behavior—whether it is on them, you, or on the team. We all have blind spots, and feedback improves self-awareness. Provide suggestions and advice and make it clear that you are looking for a positive outcome.

Most people react positively when the feedback is constructive and devoid of subjective statements or generalizations. But when you present feedback as a characterization of a personality trait, you can expect folks to get defensive.

Assume the Best

As a leader, assume you are dealing with *a good person* who simply exercised *bad judgment*. **There's a huge difference between being a *bad person* and being a *poor performer.***

Great moms understand the subtlety. They know better than to say to their child, "You are rude," or "You are careless." Instead, they'll say, "That answer was rude," or "You *appeared* careless." The former conveys a state of permanency while the latter isolates the behavior to a moment in time, therefore leaving the door open for improvement.

"There are no bad people … just some who haven't had access to a good education."
Thérèse to Elise
Château-Gaillard, France

Let Them Drive the Process

Talking about improvement, your role as a leader is to help your team turn things around. Suggest solutions, tools, or resources, if need be, but **leave it to the team member to come back with an action plan.** It is up to them to identify what they can do to change things. Then, hold them accountable. Their change of behavior should not be contingent on you doing extra work on their behalf.

Think about it this way: When a child is late getting ready for school every morning, moms have two options. They can get up earlier, prepare their child's clothes, backpack, and breakfast, prod and nudge them repeatedly, and monitor every move so they can get them out of the house on time. This will work, but at the mom's expense, and it isn't sustainable.

Moms know that the better option is to propose an earlier wake-up time, recommend the child lays out their clothes the night before, suggest a to-go breakfast, and then simply let the chips fall where they may—even if it means showing up to school with mismatched clothes, looking disheveled, or being hungry. They might even be missing some homework, their lunchbox, or their gym bag—a small price to pay to learn about organizational skills.

Let Them Face the Music

Sometimes, experiencing the consequences makes the lesson impossible to forget. One Friday when Jullian was in fifth grade, his teacher sent me a message saying that he had failed to turn in an important assignment. She explained she was reluctant to fail him—on account of his charming self, no doubt—and she would extend the due date until Monday, providing he turned in his assignment first thing that morning.

I called her right away and begged her to please give him an F. My request surprised her, and she pointed out that most parents frowned upon teachers who gave Fs. I was adamant that he should learn accountability above all else, so she reluctantly complied.

Though Jullian's grade point average took a big hit that semester, he learned the lesson the hard way. From that time on, he turned in all his assignments on time. (Or at least *most* of them . . .)

As uncomfortable as confronting issues and giving feedback may be, you must be specific about potential consequences should someone fail to meet the expectations you have laid out for your team. More importantly, you need to **follow through**.

Be ready to enforce said consequences. Observe your team member in the days or weeks that follow. Always close the loop on the conversation by either praising noticeable changes or moving on to disciplinary action if the behavior continues.

If delivered respectfully and supported with facts, feedback can be the wake-up call that steers people to better performance.

As for the night I didn't let my parents know I wouldn't be home for dinner, my mom was clear about the possible consequences. You can bet your bottom dollar she was going to follow through. So from that day on, while I lived under my parents' roof, I never forgot to let them know my whereabouts. This meant that I never had to pay rent. Mom's lesson was both memorable and priceless.

———

In my life and my career, I remember every encounter with people who have given me candid and constructive feedback. Even though it stung a bit, I am truly grateful for the gift they bestowed on me.

Personally, I never enjoyed perpetually policing my team or my children, but it comes with the territory. As they say, if you can't take the heat, get out of the kitchen . . . In other words, if you're not willing to give feedback, you shouldn't be in a leadership position.

Fortunately, there are far more enjoyable tasks that await you. On the other side of the feedback coin, there is recognition—something we all crave and never tire of, something that fuels performance and moves the team to greatness.

10

Bravos and Encores

———

My dad, Victor, came from a low-income family where compliments were rare. In their home, children were expected to study hard while helping with household chores even at a young age. By the time they were fourteen, children were expected to take on a side job to further support the family. None of that was considered worthy of praise or recognition. It was just normal.

As a result, Dad was a man of few words, and words of praise did not come easy for him. When I graduated from high school a year early, I rushed home eager to tell my parents the news. My dad's only comment was, "This is for your own good."

Though he was not wrong on principle, I was disappointed that he didn't show any pride in my achievement. It was a bittersweet moment for me. Mom was quick to fill the gap. She was over the moon for me and let it be known to anyone willing to listen.

Mothers understand better than anyone children's need for recognition. They have an innate ability to make a child feel important, appreciated, and loved. From the moment a mother first holds her baby in her arms, she shares words of affirmation with the baby. This fosters a deep sense of security and belonging, especially with young children.

Beyond these demonstrations of love, moms often show appreciation for their kids' behaviors. They all intuitively understand how praise and recognition contribute to building a child's self-esteem. So they will keep that front and center and dispense loving comments, compliments, and encouragement day after day.

"Always be your beautiful self."
Jill to Alyse
New Orleans, LA, USA

Sometimes, though, there can be too much of a good thing. I realized that once I witnessed the American approach to parenting and could compare it with what I had experienced in France. Bear with me.

While French parents tend to administer words of praise sparsely, Americans put praise on steroids. They spontaneously and generously dispense all manner of recognition—cheers, high fives, even awards.

In America, parents often treat kids like royalty. Every achievement, each milestone—no matter how small—calls for a celebration and is duly hailed, lauded, acclaimed, documented, and shared for the world to marvel at. "Look! It's their first rollover . . . first word . . . step . . . tooth . . ."

Then come the school milestones. In France, kids only formally graduate from high school and college. Not so in America. Here, kids also have graduation ceremonies to mark the completion of kindergarten and middle school too. And every graduation calls for celebration.

Parenting in America seems to imply living in a perpetual state of adulation for our kids, glorifying their achievements while fire-hosing oohs and aahs, kudos, and words of praise.

And then there are athletic feats, a whole other tier of celebration. I've spent enough time on the sidelines at soccer games to have witnessed firsthand the extent to which some parents go to celebrate their kids' exploits and prowess with an unending spitfire of superlatives. Not to mention the fact that every team player seems to be given trophies, because "Everyone's a winner!"

Now, you think I am either exaggerating or being cynical, don't you? Don't get me wrong. I wholeheartedly believe in recognition and praise. And admittingly, after I moved to the US, it wasn't long before I joined in with superlatives of my own. After all, I didn't want my kids to feel underappreciated. But the reality is that parents often dish out praise and recognition without rhyme or reason. In the end, **this constant stream of praise drowns out what is *actually* important**.

It is true that encouraging kids is crucial to building their self-esteem. But if they get a sense that the encouragement is cheap or disingenuous, or if we lead them to believe that they can do no wrong, there is danger.

Picture a cohort of teenagers raised on a diet of praise and compliments entering the workforce with their inflated egos and sense of abilities. Now imagine them failing at their first assignment or even their first job. That's a mighty steep fall to recover from, especially since their mothers likely aren't there to hold their hands.

The plain truth and negative feedback are painful. Negative feedback is even more brutal when you've never been told that, sometimes, you don't meet expectations, sometimes you aren't good enough, sometimes you fail . . . and it is OK. It is a part of life.

So how do mothers prepare their kids for this reality? They focus their recognition on the effort and the journey, not on the outcome. Great moms focus on catching kids trying hard, putting effort into their tasks, failing, and trying again.

They catch kids taking initiative and doing something good. They catch them being resilient, resourceful, and attempting to problem-solve on their own. They catch them drawing the lessons from failure and devising a better approach for next time. Mothers know that these are the skills and behaviors that will serve them well in life.

And when they witness any of these happening, mothers reinforce and validate these behaviors. And *that* is the right time for praise.

"You worked really hard on your project. Good job."

"You didn't give up on your math problem and worked at it on your own. Well done!"

"All your practicing is paying off. You never gave up. I'm proud of you."

See? The emphasis is on the effort, not the outcome.

When children understand specifically what triggers words of praise, ***they repeat the behavior.*** And yes, the praise makes them feel good. But that is the "outcome" of recognition, not the "purpose."

Moms understand that *their own satisfaction* should not be the yardstick by which kids should measure their accomplishments.

They know that their praise is most effective when comments start with *you* rather than *I*.

"You made the right decision under pressure" instead of "I am proud of you for making the right decision under pressure."

"You showed resilience when things got tough" instead of "I am so impressed by how resilient you were."

Self-esteem doesn't grow because of praise. Self-esteem grows when kids see they can improve, that they are able, relevant, and can make a positive difference.

Great moms let kids know when they do good and keep their praise proportional to the achievement. They hold the "big guns" for the "big ones" to make sure recognition remains credible and meaningful. (Sorry kids, but setting the dinner table does not qualify for a medal or a round of applause!)

Mothers **calibrate their praise** based on how the achievement matters in the big scheme of things, and always, always, ***attach it to a specific behavior***.

> "How much do I love you? A bushel and a peck and a hug around the neck!"
> Carmen to Mary
> Orlando, FL, USA

When we dispense encouragement with all this in mind, kids demonstrate the right behaviors not because they have to, but because they understand *it is the right thing to do*.

———

Not being relevant is what haunts every one of us. People just want to know they matter. If you were to ask a homeless person what is most difficult, they may tell you it isn't poverty, it's feeling invisible, irrelevant. The same goes for an organization. People want to know that they belong, they matter, they contribute effectively, and they move the needle.

As a leader, it's your job to make sure your team knows they matter. And there is no better way than by showing appreciation when they do something right.

Much like moms share words of affirmation and appreciation with their kids, your team and partners need to know you love and appreciate them.

We rarely talk about love in the workplace, but great leaders care, support, develop, trust, and focus on their team members—all demonstrations of love. They convey that they value the individual above and beyond job performance.

"Be kind. Take care of others. It will come back tenfold as people will remember that more than any responsibilities you had."
Sharon to Jenna
Orlando, FL, USA

By the way, **being nurturing and loving does not mean you are weak.** Quite the opposite, in fact. It takes a strong and confident individual to express care and compassion. It is an expression of our humanity.

You should not shy away from demonstrating love in the business world. Here's how.

Share Genuine Words of Affirmation

No matter what their level of responsibility is, let your team members know you value them, and that their contributions matter to the success of the team.

Don't be vague, though. Outline *precisely* how they impact the end result for the organization. Elevate their contribution by showing them how it fits in the overall product or service you deliver as a team. Better yet, make this a foundational part of their onboarding. As soon as they join your team, make sure team members know their role is important to the success of your organization.

Don't stop at onboarding. Spontaneously and frequently continue to call out successes. But don't go overboard. Just like kids can smell a fake a mile away, so can your team.

By being specific and sincere with your affirmations, you foster a sense of security and belonging, and you convey that your team members are as valuable as anyone else in the organization. It may not seem like much to you, but unsolicited compliments mean the world to them.

Target Specific Desired Behaviors

When dispensing praise and recognition, focus on specific desired behaviors. You will not only celebrate but also reinforce said behaviors. And that's the idea because whether you're five or forty-five, you will repeat a behavior when someone recognizes and appreciates it.

Dr. Goldie, our kids' orthodontist in Orlando, understood this well. His practice dispensed tokens to the kids who had done a good job brushing their teeth and those who showed up on time for their appointment. The kids could exchange the tokens for a prize ranging from simple trinkets to movie tickets. And the winners' names would appear on the bulletin board for all to see.

So not only did our kids scrupulously brush their teeth—quite a miracle in itself—but they would pester me to get them to their appointment on time. Voilà! Identify the outcome you desire and recognize the appropriate behavior.

It's no different in the professional environment. When you notice something done right, recognize and reward it. And if you want it to become common practice, highlight the behavior and communicate the what, the who, and the how to your team. **Describe the situation, the behavior, and the outcome** with specifics. When you do so, you paint a vivid picture of what great behavior looks like.

Not only will the beneficiary understand precisely what they did right, but so will others. The hope is that they will choose to emulate the behavior.

This certainly worked with my kids. When I praised Margot, then seven, for making her bed, Tristan, three years her junior, rushed to his room and gathered his covers and sheets in one great big clump atop his bed, hoping to elicit similar praise. Though the results were undoubtedly messy, we gave him an A for effort. (The American way of parenting seemed to have rubbed off on me.)

> *"I won't complain if my daughter wants to eat more broccoli."*
> Marisza to Vanessa
> Montréal, Canada

In the same way, when you see something done right, broadcast it. Leverage this example to encourage the rest of the team to follow suit.

There's No One-Size-Fits-All

Your team members have distinct personalities. Figure out what works for each person. Drawing from my parenting playbook, I can attest to the fact that each child requires a different approach. Some kids need public validation, others shy away from the spotlight. Some need physical displays of affection. Others—especially boys in their teenage years—will recoil at the mere thought of it!

Some children react positively to an act of kindness. Others object to the slightest intrusion into their personal world and just want to be left alone. Young ones want attention and quality time. Teenagers cherish their freedom and would rather you recognize them by giving them more independence.

Much of that applies to your team. To each their own. So pay attention to their verbal and non-verbal cues to identify what each team member values most. Better yet, ask them.

Some may relish the spotlight; others dislike being singled out—even positively. Certain individuals would rather you provide them with quality one-on-one time than be publicly put on a pedestal. Some simply need words of appreciation. Others don't care for praise; they would rather you acknowledge what they did great and put your money where your mouth is.

Show Me the Money

This brings me to another point: gift giving and monetary compensation. There is a time and place for this, but we often grossly overestimate the long-term impact.

Don't get me wrong. We all enjoy making more money, and we all work to earn as much as possible. For some, paychecks barely cover basic needs and there is sometimes "too much month" left at the end of their money.

But once individuals can take care of their basic needs, receiving a raise or bonus has a very limited impact on behavior *in the long term.*

Consider Christmas morning when you shower kids with gifts and presents. Their happiness barometer is high. But by the time you have cleared the house of all the wrapping paper, the excitement has already died down. The next day, the new toys are still a hot commodity, but the previous day's euphoria has faded. Three days later, the toys are part of the domestic landscape; the glee is over, and the kids have moved on to coveting the next thing.

Such can be the impact of a pay raise or bonus. Inevitably, we adjust our spending to the new level of income. The satisfaction dies down fast because there is always a new toy or new shiny object lurking. Over time, the pay raise is but a distant memory washed out by a craving for more.

For sustained satisfaction, look to **provide your team members with a strong sense of relevance** beyond monetary compensation. Highlight how their contribution matters to the project and the company at large.

Keep It Simple

No matter how well you understand the importance of praise and recognition, we all too often relegate it to the back burner. More pressing matters seem to take precedence. Some leaders confine themselves to overly structured and formal recognition programs such as Employee of the Month, then assume their job is done.

These programs are often derided, for they are devoid of spontaneity and can even seem disingenuous. That's why I believe that the most effective forms of recognition are simple words of appreciation dispensed every day, be it verbally or in writing. It also is the most genuine.

Thank you for your contribution to this project. You are a big part of our success.

That's it. No need to overcomplicate.

Keep in mind that the things people really desire are love, strong connections, and a purpose. In an organization, all of this translates into a sense of belonging, relevance, and achievement and it generates a lot of goodwill from your team members.

As a leader, your role is to nurture this goodwill and keep them loyal, engaged, and motivated. When in doubt, just remember that no one has ever said, "Enough already. I get way too much recognition. I can't stand it!"

———

Recognition, much like feedback, requires intentionality. Both must be featured prominently in the organization's culture, and that is something that, yet again, falls squarely on the shoulders of the leader.

Much like the best intentions, the best processes, or the best initiatives, recognition and feedback won't make a significant difference unless they are part of purposeful and well-thought-through communication.

11

Can You Hear Me Now?

———

I f you were to ask mothers to name their biggest frustrations, I'll bet communication would be right up there, that feeling that much of what they say is lost in space, that they're talking to a wall.

Still, mothers have successfully passed down directives, recommendations, insights, and wisdom for generations. How? They operate like master anglers. Hear me out.

First, they know which fish they're going for. In other words, they know their audience. They understand that you cannot talk to a five-year-old the way you address a teenager or even a husband (though the latter is debatable). They customize their message to each child to ensure they assimilate the information. Mothers know that kids have distinct personalities and will each respond in their own way.

I learned to pay attention to how each of my kids would respond to the way I communicated with them. Jullian would often not acknowledge my message, yet he'd be able to quote me verbatim weeks—if not months—later. If he disagreed, he'd debate

me openly and argue about the need, the accuracy, or the rationale
of his view. He was my challenger, so I had to come prepared for
a robust discussion.

Margot, on the other hand, would ask a million questions
because she found comfort in having details. She disliked surprises
or vague messages. She had to know why, what, how, and when.
She was my detail gatherer. I knew to wait until I had all the information available before communicating with her.

As for Tristan, he would hardly respond to verbal communication and was usually happy to just go with the flow. He was my
observer. When confronted with something new, he had to see
or experience it to internalize, learn, or retain it. Repetition and
patience were key.

Not only do mothers customize their message according to
the recipient's personality, but they also take timing into consideration. There are times when a child is not receptive or maybe too
emotional. Moms wait for the appropriate time to ensure that the
message reaches its destination, much like anglers increase their
chances of a successful catch by avoiding windy weather, knowing
full well that waiting for calmer waters will make it easier to notice
when the fish has taken the bait.

Mothers also consider the location. They tend to have a favorite "fishing hole" where they can reliably expect to be successful
in delivering the message. It may be the car ride home with their
teenagers or a young child's bedroom as they tuck them in for the
night.

If the fish doesn't bite, mothers will sometimes resort to chumming the waters with a bit of reverse psychology. The idea is not
to be deceptive but to provide kids with a choice. This is a far cry
from the authoritative "my way or the highway." Chumming the
waters can sound like this: "You don't want to eat your dinner?

That's OK. It's time for bed then." Or, "You don't want to share your toys? No problem. I guess the play date's over."

When dealing with a defiant teenager, mothers sometimes opt for, "I can't make you do this. You decide what is best for you." That effectively puts the teenager in the driver's seat and recasts the conversation toward their autonomy, which is what they crave most.

Mothers understand that communication is a two-way street, and there needs to be a reaction in the form of a verbal response, an action, or a change in behavior. It can be immediate or may require more patience. After all, you seldom get a bite as soon as you cast your line.

So they keep their eyes on the line, and they watch the connection. When they sense the communication lines are open, they put away the electronics, quiet their mind, and listen attentively.

With so many distractions at our fingertips, it's easy to miss an opportunity when it presents itself. That coveted tug on the line may be subtle, and if you're not paying attention, you may miss it altogether.

Alternatively, when you feel a response on the other end of the line, you may have a knee-jerk reaction and engage right away. Moms, like expert anglers, understand that it is actually time to pause and let the fish come to them. They stop, watch, and listen before talking again.

This is especially important when addressing a critical matter or guiding a potentially consequential decision. In that case, kids need to be provided with time to internalize a message, understand its implication thoroughly, and gather their thoughts.

Eventually, the message makes its way to its destination. The fish may nibble the line and moms notice just a gentle tug at which point they proceed delicately, especially when dealing with teenagers. Remember, the fish hasn't taken the bait . . . yet.

Moms know not to reel in too quickly because they may either pull the hook right out of the fish's mouth or the line may snap, and the fish will swim away with hooks, rigs, and lures. Instead, mothers may give a little line and steadily reel back in, let go, then reel back in again. This way, they tire the fish out. Perseverance is the name of the game.

Successfully landing a fish requires both patience and repetition. Moms know that being smooth and consistent will yield the best results. Eventually, they will get the outcome they were hoping for.

I am no master angler, but as a mother, I understand this basic principle: You can land a great catch and be successful if you know exactly where, when, and how to hook a fish. The same can be said in any situation that requires effective communication.

———

Considering we all spend much of our time staring at tools of communication, you'd think we'd all be expert communicators by now. Au contraire! While phones and internet access have made communication faster and easier, it has done no such thing for improving the quality of our messages. Not that our messages are all bad; there are just too many of them, and this dilutes their impact.

So you face a serious dilemma. You must ensure communication gets through without clogging the airwaves with too much of it.

Ironically, every job requirement lists "exceptional communication skills" as a prerequisite, yet few individuals or organizations can describe what that looks like. Why? Because it varies depending on the context, the timing, the messenger, the audience, the message itself, and the circumstances.

With so many variables, leaders—like mothers—must proceed with intent and a structured approach.

Consider Whom You Are Trying to Reach

Sometimes, you might cast a very wide net and broadcast messages companywide for fear of missing someone. But this results in bloated mailboxes, overwhelmed team members, and a vast quantity of emails that are barely scanned, let alone read. This is especially true in big organizations with many cross-functional projects.

Using the angler analogy, consider the fish you're after. Shift your perspective to put yourself in their fins and identify the format that is most appropriate to reach that group.

Considering that your team includes people who will respond to different bait, ask yourself: *What method should I choose to reach them individually? Is it a simple memo? A face-to-face conversation? A team meeting? A town hall? What level of detail and frequency do they require? Must I be the one who delivers the message in person?*

Pressured by time, we too often settle for the most convenient to us or the most expedient, but this does not make it effective.

Create structure in your communication, much like you would any other process. **And when you implement a specific communication protocol, be diligent about using it**. Too often, leaders cut corners and jump a few steps simply because they can. In doing so, they create mass confusion and frustration. Use the agreed-upon channels and the communication procedures you want to see practiced in your organization.

Create an Information Hub

In some instances, I have found that an effective way to pass down information is to narrow the audience down to a select few employees, then assign them the responsibility of keeping their team up to speed.

Think of such a group as a communication hub that centralizes all information and reports back out to their peers or departments. Its members do not have to be department or project leaders. In fact, this type of assignment is ideal for empowering a promising employee who is ready for added responsibilities.

Whenever I'd communicate information this way, I could easily check that the message was reaching the right audience by checking in with the team members standing at the end of the receiving line. If the message had either not reached the right people or been distorted, I could call it out before it became an issue.

Delegating communication responsibilities presents the added benefits of creating an environment of trust, fostering collaboration, and developing the chosen team member, not to mention freeing up valuable time on your calendar.

Prevent Death by Meeting

How many times have you found yourself in a meeting wondering, *Why am I here? Is there a way to communicate this information more effectively than yet another meeting?*

If you find you are constantly shooting the breeze, getting off topic, tackling side issues irrelevant to half of the people in attendance, rambling, or, worse yet, noticing participants being buried in their phones and tending to other matters, wonder no more. These are symptoms of unproductive meetings. The onset of this chronic condition is slow, but the symptoms get worse over time.

Big organizations are particularly susceptible to death by meeting. If there is no debate, valuable discussion or decision-making involved, and if you can't walk away with a decision or an action plan understood by everyone, it probably wasn't worth your time. Too often, we are reluctant to pull the plug on these "zombie" meetings because they are part of an established routine and attendees simply keep showing up. Such meetings are mere data-dumping sessions. Shorten them or get rid of them altogether.

Meetings should take as little time or as long as you need to reach a specific objective. Ever heard of Parkinson's Law? It claims that the amount of work expands to fill the time available for its completion. If you schedule an hour-long meeting, it will last an hour. If you schedule only twenty minutes, you'll complete your discussion in that amount of time.

To prevent going down a slippery slope, be disciplined about creating *and following* an agenda. This way, everyone can be prepared to contribute to the discussion, but they are limited to the issues that require everyone's input or advice. If a topic is only relevant to a couple of individuals, it can be tabled until the end of the meeting or a later occasion when a smaller committee can address it.

Virtual Meetings 101

With the onset of the pandemic, we've all had to rely on Zoom calls and other virtual meeting platforms. Over time, I've noticed what works and what doesn't. I won't get into the technical aspect of it as I am no Zoom wiz, but there are some basic rules of etiquette that make these meetings more efficient and user-friendly.

For starters, mute your mic until you are ready to speak. No one is interested in hearing your dog barking or whatever background noise emanates from your household.

Then, use the hand-raising feature to let others know you want to contribute. This prevents participants from speaking over each other.

Consider assigning an emcee who can facilitate participation by monitoring hand-raising, assigning speaking turns, and monitoring the chat function.

One last comment: Turning off your camera tells me you're doing something else. It shows that you have disconnected from the group and think you have more valuable tasks to tend to. If the meeting is concise and there is a clear agenda relevant to all attendees, there's no reason this should be acceptable. So, unless there is a valid reason like a slow connection or you've let the group know that you're about to gobble up your lunch and want to spare them the visual, turn on your camera and pay attention. (Glad I got that off my chest!)

When Possible, Opt for In-Person Conversations

A simple face-to-face allows you to respond to immediate concerns or questions without having to deal with back-and-forth communication. Not only does this eliminate many emails, but there is also less room for misinterpretation as the tone of voice and body language will convey what the words cannot do.

If a matter is important to you, addressing it in person will also carry more weight than a memo or an email.

When you have a one-on-one, turn off your phone and put it away. Be present. Listen intently. Do not look over your interlocutor's shoulder, and for crying out loud, do not glance at your phone. You may have a million other things on your mind, but this is possibly your team member's only opportunity to address concerns or discuss things that matter to them. Focus on that conversation and show them you care by giving your undivided attention.

By the way, the same goes for when you are on the phone. If you think you can do something else while listening—or pretending to listen—think again! Unless it is a totally mindless activity, people can tell that they don't have your full attention.

Be to the Point, Be Brief, Be Seated

Don't cover too much ground with a single message. If your communication style is to firehose people, know that most of your message is lost in the ether. Mothers know that all too well, so they use simple messages and repetition. When a teenager reaches for the car keys, they fire off a quick, "Drive safely, and wear your seat belt."

In the same way, leaders must streamline their message. For instance, if you're pushing a customer service initiative, pick *one* behavior to incorporate into your outgoing communication until it is fully integrated into the company culture. Then move on to the next behavior. To keep everything top of mind, continue to address these behaviors on a rotating basis.

Let It Sink In

You may have been thinking about an issue for a while, but when you deliver the message, it may be the first time your team hears about it. Too often, leaders assume that because the communication is out there, their team has received the message. Big mistake.

When a mother tries to get her kids' attention while they're watching TV, she knows it takes more than one attempt to unglue them from the screen. Assume the same with your team. You may think you're done communicating, but the message has not sunk in yet. They are just starting to internalize the information.

This is especially true when a leader introduces a new process or brings important change to the organization. Consider your new initiative and think of it as a departing train. Some team members (usually a small minority) will jump on right away, eager to get to the destination. Lean into them to spread the word and win over the rest of the team members.

Meanwhile, the vast majority (the skeptics) will wait to see how the change will affect them personally. They will eventually come aboard on their own time and terms once they fully comprehend the scope of the initiative.

During this time of transition, leaders must deliver the message personally to add their weight to the initiative and ensure that communication is consistent, timely, and accurate. There will always be a few stragglers and reluctant team members who keep an agenda of their own and resist change. They might even try to sabotage the initiative with confusing or conflicting messages. These individuals may eventually board the train but on their own terms. Some never will, and you'll have to address this as a performance issue.

> "Do not confuse speed with haste."
> Elise to Sandrine
> Quévert, France

Communicating in times of change requires that you invest time, effort, and repetition so everyone gets on board.

Keep Your Ear to the Ground

Once you've taken care of the outbound message, it's time to pay attention to the inbound. Much like with teenagers, leaders sometimes feel most of the conversations happen through a closed door.

If you're talking *at* people and never provide a channel for them to respond, chances are the door will remain closed. So limit the lectures. Those will just fall on deaf ears and will result in eye-rolling or a collective shrug.

Be intentional about **putting in place two-way channels of communication.** Invite your team to provide feedback, and as stated before, don't be vague about your expectations. Be specific about what you want to know, what you are interested in hearing, the level of detail you expect, and with what frequency.

If there is no inbound communication coming forth, do not assume that all is well in the world. Moms know that when kids are overly quiet, something is brewing. When you sense you may not be getting all the information you need or your team is reluctant to share, engage and **ask open-ended, probing questions**. At first, you may just get a vague answer, but with persistence, you may get to the bottom of whatever is on their mind. (I managed to put the kibosh on a few of my kids' shenanigans with this approach.)

As you look for input, make sure that you're reaching out to all levels of the organization and in all directions.

It's amazing how easily you can resolve simple issues if the communication works both ways. During my weekly walk-throughs at Walt Disney World, I always tried to engage with the retail team members. One of my favorite go-to questions was always a version of, *In your role, is there something that frustrates you that I can help you resolve?* This is how I discovered an issue that had been an ongoing frustration for quite a while.

At the time, the retail team at the German Pavilion was receiving dozens of daily guests' requests for chocolate Kinder Eggs—highly popular in Germany, yet nowhere to be found at Epcot. This was a missed opportunity, and the retail team couldn't understand the buyer's oversight. They lamented their requests had been falling on deaf ears for too long.

I made note of the retail team's complaint and remembered to address the request with the buyer at our next meeting.

Somehow, this buyer never gave this issue much of a second thought. In her view, considering the scope of her responsibilities, she had many more pressing issues to address. However, she was surprised when I shared the sheer number of daily requests that came in, and she realized why this was a matter of great frustration for the German cast members at Epcot.

She proceeded to explain that the Kinder Eggs did not pass US safety regulations as they contained a small toy that kids could accidentally swallow. The bottom line: We could not sell Kinder Eggs on Disney property, no matter what.

Turns out the matter had simply been lost in translation and had drowned in the sea of back-and-forth communication.

I went back to Epcot to deliver the message. You would think I had declassified a highly sensitive piece of information! All it took was for me to listen to both parties on either side of the merchandise division, then pass on the *complete* information to the *appropriate* person.

No one had ever elevated the issue properly, and no one had ever communicated the reason, thus creating frustration between both partners. A simple issue like this can quickly damage a working relationship or jeopardize someone's credibility.

Be Willing to Hear What You Don't Want to Hear

For effective communication to take place, be willing to hear the truth and nothing but the truth, whether it is coming from team members or customers.

Make it safe for them to voice frustrations and concerns or ask for assistance. I have always told my teenagers that they could call me whenever they needed help—no questions asked, no justification needed, and no consequences to fear.

For a leader, it may be worth taking a step back and asking yourself: *What mechanisms have I put in place to let the flow of information come back to me? Am I approachable and accessible? Am I visible? Do I keep office hours when I am available to my team members? Is there a way for people to reach me anonymously? Can my team leave me personal voice-mail messages? Do I regularly host team feedback sessions? Do I thank my team members for their communication regardless of its value? And how do I react when presented with bad news or negative feedback?*

These are all excellent questions, tools, and tactics you can implement to encourage back-and-forth communication.

Make Sure the Communication Has Landed

Finally, evaluate the impact and effectiveness of communication by assessing the results. Measure how much has been retained by asking probing questions at different levels of the organization. This way, you can see who knows what.

Ever heard your mom ask, "What did I just say?" She, too, wanted to make sure the message had landed. When you ask collaborators at the end of the line to deliver the message back to you, you can determine if it has morphed as it traveled through the maze, much like in children's game of telephone.

Until your message lands as intended, you need to keep broadcasting it, making it simple, purposeful, and therefore memorable.

———

On a recent visit to New Orleans, I noticed a sign above the sink in the ladies' room at the airport. It said, "Wash your hands like you ate crawfish and need to put your contacts in."

I chuckled and complied. The message was funny, themed to the location, and memorable.

Why was this so effective? When communication triggers an emotional response—be it surprise, laughter, sadness, or pride—we retain it. This supports the idea that leaders should never overlook one of the most powerful ways to communicate: storytelling.

12
Once Upon a Time . . .

———

My mom, Anna, was born in 1932 in a rural area near Lyon, France, and was seven years old when World War II started. Germany invaded in May 1940—just a few days before Mom's eighth birthday—and forced the French government to surrender. As a result, French people lived under German control and had to comply with stringent food and fuel rationing.

By 1943, some of the French railway workers had joined the Resistance and helped sabotage infrastructure whenever and wherever possible. My grandfather was among those brave men. During the Resistance, he would sporadically show up in the middle of the night to see his family but lived mainly in hiding with his fellow Resistance fighters.

With no father to rely on, their family did not have many resources. Food was scarce, as basic ingredients like milk, meat, and potatoes were redirected to the German army. Everyone tried to make ends meet by growing food and foraging whatever they could.

While I was growing up, Mom would sometimes share memories of the war. She'd talk about how they cooked with lard if they were lucky to get any, ate root vegetables or cabbage most days, and never saw an ounce of sugar or chocolate the entire duration of the war.

Mom would often talk about the liberation of France and how she and other kids mustered the courage to go visit the American troops on a nearby battlefield after they had soundly defeated the then-retreating German forces. She spoke of a kindhearted American soldier who gave her a teaspoon of sugar which she carried carefully in her pocket all the way back home to her mom. It was a commodity too precious to lose.

The next day, another soldier gave her a piece of Hershey's chocolate from the US Army K-rations—a heavenly treat for a child who had just endured five years of rationing.

Once the occupation ended, things improved slowly. Still, Mom remembered how the first Christmas after the war, she and her siblings were each given a single present: an orange. To this day, Mom claims she can still taste the combined sweetness and tanginess of that orange which she ate piece by piece over several days.

Mom's stories painted a vivid picture of life during the occupation. I'd be distressed when she described the unfair restrictions they had to live with and moved to tears knowing that she experienced this as a child. When she'd describe her joy while tasting something as simple as sugar, chocolate, or an orange, I swear I could almost taste it too.

I have heard these stories many times, and they occupy a special place in my heart. I think of Mom when I see a Hershey bar, and to this day I still reluctantly throw away food, knowing she would disapprove.

Those stories are memorable not only because they are part of my family's heritage, but also because they always elicit an emotional reaction. And the more emotional we get, the more we can relate and the more we remember.

Mothers understand that. They connect with their kids through storytelling and pass on knowledge and values from one generation to another. This is nothing new.

For centuries, culture has been passed down in similar ways, whether through cave paintings, books, or orally around a campfire. And nowadays we have a myriad of options at our fingertips, thanks to technology. **The outcome of a compelling story is always the same: It sticks in our collective memory.**

> *"When you can't have what you like, you must like what you have."*
> Leona to Elise
> Fouras-les-Bains, France

In my case, my mother's stories taught me about resilience and courage, about not taking anything for granted, about enjoying the small things, and about kindness.

———

Sometimes stories are just the product of our imagination, but they can convey a memorable message with just as much intensity as if they were real.

When my kids were young, bedtime was by far my favorite time of day. I'd finally get to kick off my shoes and snuggle with them. All three of my children had a bedtime ritual that included story time.

Tristan was fond of the Berenstain Bears stories, and Jullian loved Dr. Seuss. When she was about six, Margot had a ritual of her own that involved telling "the story of the bed." I do not recall how this story came to be, but here is how we told it—with great emphasis for dramatic effect.

"Centuries ago, families would lie down wherever they could and sleep on the ground. Years later, they'd settle in dwellings and would sleep on pallets made of hay. Someone eventually thought to put the hay in a sack and raise it to protect it from the cold and humidity. This was how the bed was invented. Next came the blanket and the pillow. Later on came the footboard and head-board so your feet and your head would not fall off at night. And eventually came 'the key' to the bed: the bedsheet! It keeps you cool when it's hot, and warm during cold nights."

This is where the story ended. At this point, Margot, who had been giddily waiting for this moment all along, would yell: "The sheet is NOT THE KEY!" We would act indignant and retort that it was indeed. After a bit of mischievous bantering back and forth, we'd finally tuck her in and turn the light off.

Dan and I often wondered why Margot liked this silly story so much. We came to realize that the repetition brought her a sense of security and that the routine comforted her. Besides, she loved acting up at the end, as we'd pretend to be dumbfounded and would leave her bedroom in dismay.

Margot is now a grown woman, but she still remembers this story fondly. Stories are like that. Even if they're light in substance, they can bring back memories and evoke moments we cherish.

Mothers understand how important this is. That's why we read books to our kids, even if our child asks for the same book night after night.

Mothers play the parts and use different voices—anything to make the story more realistic or more relatable. They use stories as teachable moments to communicate values and insights. They understand that a good tale can help children explain their own feelings as it provides them with an emotional benchmark.

Books not only entertain and stretch one's imagination, but they also teach children about life in all its beautiful diversity.

Besides, a love for stories turns a child into an avid reader, and children who love to read grow up with a better vocabulary. This further helps them become better learners and will eventually impact their entire education. A great education can allow them to have a career of their choosing and more opportunities—part of the long-term plan mothers are fiercely determined to carry out.

That is why they use storytelling to share a powerful insight or convey an important message to their children.

———

I once read *The End of Poverty*, in which Jeffrey Sachs introduced the Millennium Development Goals. As a leader of the MDG, Sachs appealed to the international community to build roads and infrastructure. Why? Because the best way to help people pull themselves out of poverty is to put education, healthcare, and trade within reach, the key drivers to growth and development.

Roads and transportation give people access to schools where their children can get educated, to hospitals when they are sick, and to markets where they can sell the goods they produce or grow.

The goal of the MDGs was to eradicate extreme poverty by 2015. That date has come and gone, yet there are still hundreds of millions of people living on less than a dollar a day.

One of the biggest obstacles to the MDG is this: No one is moved to invest in infrastructure. A request for road funding does not stir anyone's imagination and, therefore, does not compel us to reach for the checkbook. We are all more likely to donate to a charity when we see pictures of children in need or hear the stories of a family having to make do without running water.

Such stories tug at our heartstrings because we can easily imagine ourselves in the same predicament. They make us react and *do something*. **Stories paint a picture and move us to action.** They energize, stir, galvanize, motivate, empower, embolden, and fire us up. And this is, in essence, what leaders should aim to do.

Nothing engages people like a good story. As a leader, you can convey your ideas and dreams, share your values and vision for the organization, bring clarity to your expectations, illustrate the behaviors you hope to see, and inspire your team to greater performance. And you can do it all through storytelling. It is one of the most powerful skills you can leverage as a leader.

Effective storytellers are skilled, witty, articulate, and eloquent. Of course, not everyone is a natural-born storyteller. Though it may not come easily, anyone can learn some basic storytelling skills.

Learn from Others, Then Practice

There are many ways to tell a memorable story. Watch skilled speakers and storytellers and see how they connect. Find someone you can practice telling your stories to so you can hone your skills. Start with topics you are passionate about. Use details to paint a vivid picture. Much like mothers do with their kids, use variation in intonation and pace to capture your audience's imagination, and keep the suspense alive until you get to the core of your message.

"Always tend your own garden."
Aida to Nouha
Beirut, Lebanon

Start With the End in Mind

In using storytelling with your team, be intentional. Think about what you hope to accomplish by telling the story. Ask yourself what you want your audience to feel, learn, and retain. Identify moments or examples that you can turn into a story that will drive the point.

Once you have defined the desired outcome, reverse engineer the process, working your way through your story to make sure it conveys the emotions you need to generate. Then deliver the message.

Make It Short and Memorable

A good story has one central takeaway, one good insight, one memorable nugget of wisdom. Focus on what is most important and make that the core of your story.

Less is more. Studies show that we retain only about 10% of what we hear. Make sure that what you share is succinct enough for your team not to zone out, and that they will remember the point of your story.

Speak From the Heart

It should be abundantly clear by now: Great leaders are genuine. Speak from the heart, be it with a personal story or an inspiring example. When you do so, you stir people's emotions, and your team will relate better.

What's more, your team members will get to know who you are and what you want for them and from them. And they will remember the core of your message. This will promote introspection and critical thinking, and it will compel your audience to act.

Before you know it, you will have inspired people to demonstrate the skills and behaviors you are hoping to see. They will have learned the lesson you have been trying to teach.

———

Leaders need to understand what mothers have known all along: **Stories go far beyond delivering life lessons. They connect people through emotions.** For fifteen years, I worked for Disney where we cultivated the power of a story not only through movies but also through the entire company culture—through guests relating their cherished Disney memories, employees sharing their passion for the company, people connecting through the power of their emotions.

Storytelling isn't exclusive to entertainment companies, though. It is a tool available to all leaders who want to inspire their teams.

However, there is one thing you must keep in mind: None of what you have done so far—setting the framework for success, training, recognizing, coaching, or communicating effectively—will make an ounce of difference if you don't practice what you preach.

The power of a story can only be matched by the power of an example. Often, actions speak louder than words.

13

I Want to Be Like You

———

I used to get wildly entertained watching my husband feed our babies. Dan would carefully spoon the baby food, and as he'd near the baby's face, he would open his mouth, hoping the baby would reciprocate. I thought that was hilarious . . . until I realized I was guilty of the same antics.

Silly, isn't it? But it works. Why? Because children are wired to mimic the people around them. This is why babies smile if you smile at them, try to stick their tongue out if you do, attempt to sing if you sing, and open their mouths if you open yours. Babies vocalize in response to their mom's baby talk and replicate their pitch variation.

If a mom sheds a tear as she drops off her toddler on the first day of childcare, the child will respond in kind. Toddlers pick up on their mom's anxiety even if they cannot possibly understand what is happening.

As they grow up, children replicate their parents' every move: mannerisms, body language, and the way they speak. Since they typically spend more time with their mothers, they will look at how she behaves, especially while dealing with others. *Is Mom welcoming, and does she engage easily with strangers? Is she withdrawn and shy? Does she like to be the center of attention, or is she more of an introvert?*

Though they don't have the words to describe what they're seeing, children pay attention to all of the above and emulate their parents' behaviors. As such, adults set the benchmark for children's social skills. The same goes for many other behaviors that children learn from watching their parents.

Do they lie or embellish the truth? Do they tend to speak badly of others, deflect responsibility for their actions, or do they hold themselves accountable for their mistakes? Do they work out and have a healthy lifestyle? Are they smokers or heavy drinkers? Are they prone to aggressive behaviors or verbal abuse?

If you have children, you *know* they are watching all these behaviors and soaking them up as the norm. Parents are the biggest influence in their children's lives, bar none.

With this in mind, I recently asked twenty-four-year-old Margot about the influence I have had on her behaviors as an adult. Her answer? She learned from me that if you stretch your legs and place your bare feet on your spouse or boyfriend's lap and wiggle your toes long enough, there is a good chance you will get a foot massage . . . Sigh! Not exactly the answer I was expecting.

Joking aside, this illustrates the dilemma at the center of being a role model. The good news is that your kids are watching you and will emulate your behavior. The bad news? Your kids are watching you and will emulate your behavior.

So how do mothers make sure kids emulate positive behaviors and not negative ones? How do we inspire our children to pick up on our best attributes rather than our idiosyncrasies and mistakes?

First, a mom must identify the behaviors she wants to teach her kids and intentionally dedicates time to doing just that. When I talk about teaching, I do not mean delivering a grand sermon or lecture. Rather, moms need to lead the way by demonstrating what they expect.

They know that to raise kids to be hard-working individuals, they need to demonstrate a great work ethic. If they hope to raise charitable kids, simply *telling them* to be generous with their time or money won't cut it. They might instead enlist their kids to join them in volunteering for community service, or they might give regularly to charity.

Moms understand that if they never pick up a book themselves, there are fewer chances their kids will become avid readers. They know that parents who adopt a healthy lifestyle increase the odds of having healthy kids.

If mothers curb their own screen time and promote family interaction, children will be more inclined to do the same and limit their social media, gaming, and TV exposure.

Do they always get it right? Of course not. And if kids notice the slightest discrepancy between what mothers *advocate* and what they *actually do*, they will call it out.

Children, particularly teenagers, can sniff out hypocrisy like bloodhounds. They will point out any transgression or shortcomings if given the chance. And if there is too big of a gap between what parents *say* and what parents *do*, teenagers move on to find another role model somewhere else, someone who reliably walks the talk.

To remain influential in their children's lives, mothers have to stay credible. To do so, one of the best things they can model is accountability. They know it is important to admit when they are wrong, to acknowledge when they have made a mistake, and to say sorry when they hurt someone's feelings. This way, children learn two valuable lessons.

First, they learn no one is perfect and we are all prone to making mistakes. Second, they learn that admitting shortcomings doesn't make you a lesser person. In fact, showing vulnerability takes courage.

In modeling accountability and being willing to share their mistakes, mothers effectively create a safe space for failure for their kids.

Mothers also understand that they are not the only role model in their kids' lives—especially in their teenage years. They keep a close eye on whom their child is looking up to—be it friends, relatives, athletes, or celebrities. *What values does this person stand for?* The answer to this question will determine whether or not a mom will encourage a relationship. However, guiding the choices of an eight-year-old is a lot easier than a sixteen-year-old. For that very reason, moms know that time is of the essence.

When kids are young, it's easy to monitor or even influence their choice of role models. So mothers highlight the values, qualities, and achievements of individuals they deem worthy, hoping to steer similar feelings in their children.

If parents often talk about the individuals they admire or the moral principles they adhere to, you can be sure their kids will be inclined to adopt the same views. That's why most children share the same political and societal beliefs as their parents. But if parents wait until adolescence before they impart their values, it may be too late. By then, they have little sway in their teenagers' decisions and have to let them exercise their own judgment.

However, if parents model the right behaviors and teach the right values early on, they can be confident that by the time their children are teenagers, they will intuitively know a smart decision from a poor one, a good influence from a bad one.

Mothers also understand that to be a respected role models and pass on certain behaviors, they must be consistent across the board. One misstep—even in an unrelated area—or a single dent in someone's integrity can jeopardize their credibility.

Case in point: There was once a National Football League quarterback whom my sons and their friends admired as an incredible athlete and role model. However, it came to light that this guy organized dog fights and bet on the outcomes. This news prompted an animated carpool conversation among the boys.

Such a carpool conversation is one of those moments when moms know to make themselves really small and really quiet while listening intently. With no input from the driver's seat, the boys soon agreed that dogfighting was a cruel practice, and this effectively discounted this athlete both as a football player and role model, regardless of his athletic abilities.

Considering the boys ranged in age from six to thirteen years old, I was proud to hear them exercise their common sense and change their minds about the individual in question. Rather than getting involved and trying to disparage their role model, it was satisfying for me to see them use *their own judgment* independently of what TV, social media, friends, I, or anyone else may say. It was proof that the right values were sinking in.

Meanwhile, I couldn't help but think about how hard it is to forge a great reputation as a role model and how quickly it can all come crumbling down.

———

Ken Blanchard says, "The key to successful leadership is influence, not authority." How do you influence people? By showing the way through your behavior. Companies have a distinct culture, just like families do. And much like parents set the tone for their kids, leaders set the example for their teams and their organizations . . . for better or for worse.

> *"A fish always starts to stink and rot from the head."*
> Rosina to Alessandra
> Milazzo, Sicily, Italy

None of the attributes of a leader will make a lick of a difference if you do not model the right behaviors. You may be a smart leader, a brilliant strategist, or a bold visionary, but none of that matters if you cannot get your team to execute the plan, deliver the project, or efficiently complete the tasks that their job requires. So how do you set your team on the right path?

Walk the Talk

Leaders set the values of an organization through their behaviors, and it trickles down from there. Do you expect excellence from your team? Be excellent. You expect people to treat customers and team members respectfully? Be respectful. You want to hold your team accountable? Start with holding yourself accountable. This is how you'll inspire people to adopt the right behaviors. It is also the most effective way to communicate expectations.

More than just listening to what you *say*, your team members are closely monitoring what you *do*.

Have you ever been in an office around 7 p.m. and found that many of your team members are also still at work? Ever sent an email late at night or on weekends and received a prompt reply from your team? You can advocate for a balanced approach to personal and professional life until you're blue in the face, but unless you model that behavior, your team will emulate *you*, not your words.

Team members get their cues from what their leader does. All eyes are on you. If you stay late, team members will conclude that doing the same is a prerequisite to performance excellence and potential advancement, no matter what you say.

The same goes for just about anything else, whether it is the way you address people, how you talk about others, your availability or lack thereof, your reliability and accountability, your work style, even the way you dress. It even pertains to how you behave outside of the organization, which leads me to my next point.

Lead by Example . . . Even if You Think No One's Watching

Let's assume your company decides to focus on workforce safety. You might ask team members to practice safe behaviors in everything they do. However, if you or other leaders drive like maniacs or come screeching through the parking lot at forty miles an hour every morning, what message does this send? Is safety really something the leaders feel strongly about? Does it really matter much to the organization? You can bet your sweet life that the safety initiative is dead upon arrival.

Team members will note the discrepancy and conclude that safety is nothing but a word tossed around or plastered on bulletin boards. Compliance will quickly wear off and behaviors will head down a slippery slope. Soon, there will be no turning back and no one will care. The integrity of the organization will take a hit and its reputation will be blemished.

> "What's good for the goose is good for the gander!"
> Joy to Erin
> St. Petersburg, FL, USA

"Do as I say, not as I do" has never worked and never will.

Now, as I said earlier, no one is perfect, and leaders make mistakes. So, to keep from blowing your reputation, it will help if you adopt the following tactics.

Make It Safe to Bring Up Inconsistencies

Team members must feel safe raising issues when there is a discrepancy between what leaders *expect* and what leaders *demonstrate*. Teenagers may not have any qualms about calling out hypocrisy, but employees do. They will hesitate for fear of compromising their careers.

Consider if you have expressively encouraged, facilitated, and welcomed such feedback. Ask yourself, *Do we have a process in place? Do we provide an opportunity for anonymous feedback? Will feedback be kept confidential? Are there really no repercussions for providing such feedback?*

If the answer is no, you're missing an opportunity to illuminate some of your blind spots, make changes, and score some credibility in the process. If you find it difficult to influence behaviors in your organization, it may just be that your actions contradict what you preach and you are unaware of it. Encourage your team members to call it out.

Model Vulnerability

When you have been made aware of a mistake you have made, be swift to admit it. Better yet, thank the team members who gave you candid feedback. Apologize publicly if needed, then make the necessary changes.

Holding yourself accountable will endear you to your team and promote trust—even if it is at the expense of your bruised ego. It will send the message that perfection isn't expected and will relieve team members' anxiety and the pressure to be flawless.

Set the Tone Early On

I related earlier how important it is to meet and interact with new team members. Being visible and accessible will allow you to set new hires on the right path. Behaviors are contagious, especially when you first join an organization.

New team members observe how things are done and what is acceptable. They read the room and emulate what they see, much like young children mimic their mothers' behaviors. You want to ensure that you expose them to the best role model possible because this is when they are the most receptive and compliant.

> "Have the honest heart
> that says, 'Yes,'
> The gratitude that says,
> 'Thank you,'
> The heart of remorse that says,
> 'I'm sorry,'
> The spirit of service that says, '
> I will do it,'
> The humble heart that says,
> 'Thanks to you.'
> Sachiko-San to Etsuko-San
> Ishinomaki, Miyagi, Japan

Finally, let's not discount the fact that being a role model may lead to unsuspected outcomes. My three kids have always spontaneously cleared the dishes and loaded the dishwasher after dinner. I've had friends ask me how we got them so well trained. Was this a chore we had assigned to them ahead of time? Was there some form of reward involved?

Truth is, we've never had to ask the kids to do this! They simply emulated what they saw being done. Dan and his dad have always taken it upon themselves to clear the table when we hosted dinner parties, so the kids naturally copied their father's and grandfather's behavior. Though it was never intentional, this behavior just trickled down to them.

A similar example happened while I worked at Disney. During my morning walk-through of the retail area I oversaw, when a store was clean and well stocked and everyone was ready for the day with their name tags on and a smile on their faces, I would say out loud for everyone to hear, "I like what I'm seeing!"

I chuckled to myself upon hearing one of the store managers utter the same quote in a similar fashion. I just loved the fact that he had picked up on it and learned to praise his team publicly.

So, whether you like it or not, you live in the spotlight, and you never know who's watching you! You're a role model 24/7. It is up to you to choose whether it will be for good or for bad.

———

Now, not only have you successfully put in place the foundation for success, but you have also learned the behaviors that will ensure that your team is engaged and can operate efficiently. However, if you think your task is complete, I have news for you: Things seldom go as planned. You are bound to hit a few bumps along the way, and obstacles are to be expected.

There are yet more skills and tactics that will help you navigate turbulent waters. Adopting and mastering these will make the difference between merely surviving and thriving. That's what we'll focus on in Part 3.

PART 3

Thriving

14
It's About Time!

———

J ulia Child once said, "The dinner hour is a sacred time when everyone should be together and relaxed."

Well, thanks Julia, and good luck with that! Every single mom will tell you that the 4 to 8 p.m. time frame is probably the most hectic one of the day. Had Julia Child raised any kids of her own, she would have gotten a taste of what most moms experience every day.

If you're a parent, you're probably nodding your head in agreement. If you're *not* a parent, allow me to give you a peek behind the curtain at what late afternoons/early evenings often look like in a home with three young children.

4:15 Pick kids up from school. Feed them a snack.

4:30 Drop off kid #1 at soccer practice. Start driving back home. Turn around because #1 forgot his water bottle in the car. Deliver water bottle and drive home.

4:55 Get kids #2 and #3 to start their homework.

5:00 Put in a load of laundry.

5:10 Track down kid #2 and extract her from one of her everlasting bathroom breaks. Send her back to the homework table.

5:20 Search for kid #3's elusive soccer shin guards.

5:35 Chase #3 out of the pantry and send him back to the homework table.

5:45 Look for kid #2's missing history book.

6:00 Pick up kid #1 from soccer practice. Drop off #3.

6:15 Drop off kid #2 at guitar practice. Head back home.

6:20 Get kid #1 to shower and start homework.

6:25 Start prepping dinner.

6:30 Run to the store to pick up the must-have poster board for a school project due tomorrow that #1 just remembered.

6:45 Prep lunch boxes for tomorrow.

7:05 Pick up kid #3 from soccer practice. On the drive home, remind husband not to forget to pick up #2 from her guitar lesson on his way home.

7:15 Continue dinner preparation. Settle an argument between kids #1 and #3. Move laundry to the dryer.

7:25 Ask #3 to set the table. Greet husband and send #2 to shower.

7:27 Ask #3 to set the table. Listen and sympathize with husband who grumbles about his day at work.

7:29 Ask #3 to set the table. Finish dinner prep.

7:30 Call all family members to the dinner table.

7:31 Call all family members to the dinner table.

7:32 Get husband off his cell phone.

7:33 Peel kid #1 from in front of the TV and kid #2 out of the shower.

7:35 Threaten to go on strike.

7:36 Sit down for dinner.

7:36 Get up to fetch the missing silverware.

7:37 Eat.

For the next twenty minutes or so, *if* we were lucky, we indeed sat together and enjoyed dinner. (As for the *relaxed* part, we're still working on it). Sigh!

Such is the life of a mother between 4 and 8 p.m. It's a mad rush to feed the family and get everyone ready for the next day. Over time, I realized there was a better way, and it came in two forms: pizza delivery and time management.

Parenting is a full-time job with late hours and tons of overtime. In fact, when you become a mom, 24/7 is the only shift available. There's no such thing as paid time off, vacation, bank holidays, or retirement. You can't fire or furlough your kids, and you definitely cannot go and exchange them. Once the die is cast, you are in it for the long run.

Elizabeth Gilbert rightly said: "Having a baby is like getting a tattoo on your face. You really need to be certain it's what you want before you commit."

Parenting permeates your *entire* schedule and throws more than the occasional wrench into your plans. There is only one of you and so much to do.

Whether they have one, two, or a dozen kids, mothers find efficient ways to get stuff done no matter where they are. So if anyone should know a thing or two about time management, it is a mother.

> "With only one tush, you cannot dance at two weddings."
> Nana Barbara to Lisa
> New York, NY, USA

If you have raised a child, you intrinsically understand that to survive, you need to be organized, and you need to plan *everything*—be it meals, outfits, errands, chores, even bathroom breaks!

I became a master at leveraging downtime on the side of athletic fields where I'd take care of emails and other tasks like business calls. I have paid countless bills while waiting for the kids, and I've even wrapped Christmas gifts in the back of my van while waiting in the carpool lane.

My kids learned to do the same. I always had scissors, scotch tape, glue, and markers so they could complete homework and put finishing touches to school projects while we were waiting on a sibling at, say, guitar lessons.

———

With time, I've identified nine "rules" of time management from a mother's perspective that have reliably worked for me. And as you can imagine, you can tweak every one of these best practices to apply in the workplace.

These are common-sense principles you might know . . . and promptly ignore. However, when you apply them in the workplace, these simple behaviors can make an enormous difference in your ability to make the best use of your time and survive the onslaught of tasks that land in your lap every day.

Rule #1: Optimize Your To-Do List

Whether you keep it on your phone, your day timer, or jot it down on a paper napkin at breakfast, a to-do list ensures that nothing falls through the cracks.

Armed with such a list, wise moms know to identify activities that can be completed together. They plan their day or week and take care of chores with great efficiency, like a natural-born industrial engineer! I, for one, would not only keep a running grocery list, but I would categorize the items based on their location in the store so that shopping would take as little time as possible.

Just like moms, most leaders have a daily to-do list that stretches far longer than the number of hours at the office. Glance at that list and see how you can **optimize your time by bundling tasks**. If you plan to do a walk-through of your operation and also have on your list to talk to a colleague about something, how about having a quick face-to-face while walking together? This way you avoid crowding each other's inbox with multiple back-and-forth emails, you spend time in your operation making yourself visible to your frontline, plus you get some exercise too!

Similarly, rather than scheduling multiple meetings with multiple groups, can you schedule one weekly open-door meeting? When I worked for the retail organization at Disney, we had a three-hour meeting every Thursday morning from 9 to noon, hosted by the three VPs of the merchandise division.

All new strategies, product lines, disruption plans, and other retail-related topics were presented, reviewed, and approved during these meetings, as all the key decision makers were in attendance. The result was a well-choreographed and highly productive session that eliminated the need for multiple smaller meetings. We all know how quickly those can fill up a calendar!

You get the gist. The idea is to optimize your time by grouping items from your to-do list that can be done together without compromising the quality or outcomes. This is a simple, yet underrated key to greater productivity.

Following this rule, you can relish in the joy of seeing a to-do list full of ticked boxes—so much so that you might add an item or two you had already completed just so you can have the satisfaction of checking them off the list too!

Rule #2: Rely on a Support System

Because they have so much on their plates, mothers have to create and rely on a support system. So they make friends fast and help each other out. They share the duties they can entrust to somebody else. Chauffeuring kids to and from school and activities is one of these.

Carpooling isn't as much a way of life as it is a mother's survival skill. Each week is like a perpetual do-si-do of kids jumping from one car to another, going from one house to the next, an unwieldy waltz of backpacks, gym bags, and lunch boxes.

"Four quarters are better than a hundred pennies. You are better off with four good friends than a hundred acquaintances."
Angie to Savannah
Pelham, GA, USA

Moms step up to the plate for one another and collectively cover the basic obligations of motherhood. There may not be pads nor helmets involved, but together "Team Super Moms" forms a defensive line against fumbling, forgetfulness, and short deadlines.

Leaders can't go it alone either. In my early years as a leader, I naively believed that leaders must know and do it all. But as my responsibilities grew, I realized that this could not be further from the truth. Leaders cannot function efficiently for very long unless they delegate some of the less important tasks.

So consider your to-do list and identify the tasks you can pass on to someone else. Likewise, consider what tasks you can automate by leveraging technology.

We all tend to cling to some activities because they are gratifying, we're good at them, or we've always taken care of them ourselves. But to use the words of a famous Disney princess, "Let it go!" Move on to more productive things.

As for any unexpected urgent issues, do *you* always have to be the one dealing with them? Could you delegate this responsibility to a team member?

Some leaders are reluctant to hand over the reins because of an inflated ego or a need for control. If that's you, I cannot help but ask, "ARE YOU CRAZY?" Think about how much time it would save you to hand off some of these time-sucking distractions. Plus, it's a perfect teaching opportunity for your direct reports to demonstrate their decision-making ability and readiness for greater responsibilities.

Rule #3: Make a Plan of Attack

When Jullian was six, Margot three, and Tristan just six weeks old, I started an annual ritual of traveling to France with the kids while Dan stayed behind for work. I knew that traveling by myself with three young children every summer would require significant preparation and a well-thought-out strategy. So, before I did any other trip preparations, I dedicated time to think through the travel essentials that would get us to our destination.

Taking the time in advance to identify all we'd need and prepare for all plausible scenarios ensured that year after year, we got to our destination relatively stress-free. Before every trip, I mentally considered every step of our journey to make sure I did not forget anything.

In my carry-on, I always had snacks for the kids and some new small toys to keep them entertained during the transatlantic flight. Plus, I had several spare pacifiers for Tristan, just in case.

And I should not forget to mention wipes, the number-one item on the list of travel essentials. Those come in especially handy when a child flips an entire tray of food over you (soda included). Don't ask me how I know that.

I also packed must-have medications in our carry-on bags as well as a change of clothing for each in case of a catastrophe along the way. I always added a trash bag since we somehow produced an insane amount of trash during long flights. Finally, I always made sure to have change in Euros so I could get a luggage cart at the airport upon arrival.

After packing everything I might need and more, I thought it would probably be a good idea to get the kids super tired before the flight, so off to the playground we'd go. My somewhat wishful thinking was that they'd be asleep soon after we had all buckled up on the plane and would only wake up upon arrival in Europe. It didn't always work out that way, but it bought me a few precious hours of peace and quiet.

Most of the time, we made it all the way to Paris without problems, though I feel I still owe some passengers an extra apology for the noise we made and the random kicks in the back of their seats. (As for the grumpy businessman flying Swissair from Geneva to New York on July 20, 2003, you know how I feel about you!)

The experience taught me that rather than rushing to pack, it paid off to pause and consider how to best prepare. This allowed me to organize our packing efficiently—I knew exactly where, say, I had packed the spare pacifiers—and ensured we had everything we needed on hand. Best of all, it helped me keep my sanity.

As a leader, you might not face a transatlantic flight with three little ones, but you face similar situations that come with a long list of tasks. Pressured by time, you may tend to dive right in and indiscriminately work your way down the list. In this manner, you fail to unearth some opportunities for greater efficiency and productivity. **You must commit time for reflection *ahead* of starting your day,** no matter how eager you may be to get started.

Don't start your day doing. Start your day planning. Investing time to assess the needs, resources, or challenges that lay ahead can be a game changer, as there will always be the business equivalent of a flying food tray or a lost pacifier.

So start your day by considering what needs to be done that day, then mentally prepare for each step. **Preparation upstream pays dividends downstream.** You may identify new tasks that need to be added before you can move forward, or you may remember to roll over some incomplete tasks from the prior day. Having a simple plan will also help improve your productivity and transition from one task to another efficiently.

Rule #4: Carve Out Time to Address Long-Term Goals

In Chapter 6, I explained the importance of having a long-term vision for your team, project, or organization and developing a strategy. Moms have a vision too. They see a future career for their kids, impressive feats, and a gratifying life. They often think about this vision to the point of driving themselves bonkers.

Am I doing the best I can? Will my kids have a fulfilling and happy life? Are they given the best chance to reach their potential? What kind of adult will they turn out to be? Am I raising them to have a healthy lifestyle? All these questions consume moms every day.

However, in business, we tend to focus on short-term goals. We operate like professional cyclists: heads down close to the handlebars to avoid resistance, gain as much speed as possible, and hopefully outdo the competition and reach the finish line (or the bottom line) ahead of everybody else.

Being focused on speed can keep you from seeing the potholes, roadblocks, or shortcuts down the road. Keeping your head down prevents you from seeing the changing environment (I'm looking at you Blockbuster) or keeps you from discovering the opportunities brought by new technology (did someone say Blackberry?). As a result, you may even underestimate the might of your competition (hello, General Motors).

The constant pressure to deliver pushes us to dedicate more time to managing in the present rather than looking to the future. It keeps us from figuring out ways to challenge the status quo and grow our business.

That's where great time management skills come in handy: Schedule windows of time that you dedicate to thinking about the future and how to best prepare for it. If you don't, I can promise you that something urgent will wiggle its way into your calendar.

By carving out time to prepare for long-term goals and do some deep thinking, you can take care of important issues *before* they become urgent.

Rule #5: Set Aside Some "Me Time"

Are you feeling tired, overwhelmed, exhausted, and yet dealing with insomnia? You may be suffering from a condition called *parenting*.

Parenting comes with really small slivers of time to eat, sleep, and relax. So mothers know they *must* allocate time to recharge their batteries, gain perspective, and think. If they don't carve these into their schedule, they effectively abdicate their well-being to the parenting cause. Eventually, it catches up with them, and then everything else unravels.

So mothers try to follow the airline safety spiel to "put your oxygen mask on first before assisting others." And yes, maybe a load of laundry doesn't get done that day, but no one's ever died from wearing smelly socks.

When mothers do not schedule some downtime for themselves, they become grumpy, exhausted, even sick. And when mom goes down, the family logistics fall to pieces. What good does that do?

Leaders are not immune to an overflowing schedule. How long do you think you can keep operating at full steam and deliver successful outcomes? Whether in your professional or personal life, my guess is that it's not as long as you think. Eventually, you'll get to the end of yourself and be too exhausted to think straight and too busy to worry about your health. You will burn out.

> *"Don't get sick ... it's boring!"*
> Judy to Sue
> Cape Town, South Africa

Nowadays, burnout is on everyone's lips and on every organization's radar screen. For years, it has been taking a toll on much of the workforce and affecting our collective productivity.

No matter your level of responsibilities, **serve yourself a cup of indulgence and be good to yourself.** Recognize that you can't be an effective leader if you're exhausted, sick, or missing in action. Regularly schedule some time to regroup and reset. Invest in your physical and mental well-being so you can be ready to face the challenges for your team, collaborators, and organization at large. Put this time in your calendar and commit to it. This is valuable time spent with yourself.

If you think self-care sounds selfish or lazy, you're sorely mistaken. Don't confuse movement with accomplishment. Simply showing up at work doesn't make you an exceptional leader, a productive person, or a reliable one. Quality outcomes do.

> *"No one else is responsible for your happiness or health but you."*
> Sunshine to Priscilla
> Chevy Chase, MD, USA

One more thing. Planning for some downtime in your schedule gives you a bit of wiggle room when something urgent pops up.

However, be mindful to protect this precious and necessary window of time like your career depends on it . . . because it really does.

Rule #6: Divide and Conquer

To divide and conquer is especially helpful when it comes to daunting tasks. The college application process is one of them. (And by the way, blink, and your sweet kids are off to college!) Taking care of all the paperwork is quite an endeavor, so it requires a process.

What saved us? Breaking this monumental task down into small chores over a long period and creating a timeline and checkpoints for deliverables. When needed, we assessed and adjusted as the project moved along. All of this contributed to easing the dreaded feeling that comes with long-term assignments.

Then we decided that instead of nagging our kids daily about their applications, we would sit down every Monday night and review the progress made. Any other time, the topic was off-limits.

So this is how it played out: As each of our kids went through the application process, our then-teenaged high school seniors would create a shared Google doc with the list of all the schools they were considering, including the location, the enrollment size, and the tuition cost. We jointly identified a few additional criteria that would influence their final selection of colleges.

Once they identified schools, we divvied up tasks and assigned each a due date. Then, during our Monday ritual, we'd review the progress made and tie up a few loose ends. These weekly meetings ensured we could provide input and proactively address potential snags while giving us an opportunity to appreciate how the applications were moving along.

These are all useful tactics, whether you apply to colleges or tackle a major project at work. The key is to **convert a big task**

into small manageable assignments and create checkpoints along the way.

By keeping the communication flowing back and forth with all the individuals involved, you give everyone the opportunity to see how the project is shaping up. As a result, they are less likely to bring up a big concern or come up with a surprise ask by the time you reach your deadline.

Rule #7: Stay on Task

Granted, this may be wishful thinking. When you're a mom, there are countless pulls and asks coming your way. I call this the squirrel effect. You're darting from one task to another, changing course (squirrel!), then rushing to the next task (squirrel!) before finishing the previous one. This multitasking often results in mistakes, omitted details, or poor-quality outcomes.

Mothers quickly learn to improve effectiveness by isolating themselves and creating a dedicated time and workspace—even if it means locking themselves in the bathroom. During this time, there are no more interruptions or distractions (no more squirrels), and they can focus on the task at hand.

As a leader, you know all too well that distractions can wreak havoc on your daily productivity. You are your own worst enemy. Something catches your eye (squirrel!) and before you know it, you're scanning some emails that have just come in, and you veer off course. Twenty minutes fly by before you resume what you were initially doing.

In following a mother's playbook, commit to focusing on the task at hand. Close your email window and turn off all notifications. You can probably survive a few hours without knowing the final score of that tennis match or the comments on your latest Instagram post.

As a best practice, you may choose to turn off push notifications when downloading new apps or use your computer's focus functionality that allows you to turn off all distractions with the push of one button. And when you need to address tasks that require deep thinking, isolate yourself and put your phone on airplane mode.

Dedicate time to reading and responding to emails, maybe one hour in the morning, a half hour before lunch, and at the end of your workday. And always opt for in-person conversations whenever possible so you don't have to deal with a chain of back-and-forth emails.

Rule #8: Conquer Procrastination

When it is time to do their homework, kids tend to vanish into the bathroom, the pantry, or to the fridge. There is suddenly an onslaught of urgent messages from friends or notifications on their phones that need to be read at once, all in a desperate attempt to delay the inevitable. So, most mothers know to give their kids a brief break to regroup and take care of their vital needs—food, drinks, and bathroom breaks—and then turn off the electronics before starting homework.

Unfortunately, adults hardly fare better than children. We never really outgrow procrastination. We may linger at the water cooler or copier, grab another cup of coffee from the coffee machine, or swing by someone's office to exchange pleasantries. As a result, we put unnecessary pressure on ourselves as the deadline looms closer. In the end, we are forced to make a mad rush for the finish line, which leaves us battered, bruised, and exhausted.

This is particularly true when we face a daunting task. If there's an assignment lurking that we particularly dread, we *will* find other tasks on our to-do list that suddenly seem more important.

It's amazing how we expand that list just so that we fill the time we should dedicate to tackle the tasks we dislike!

Sheer willpower and the discipline to get started aren't enough to conquer procrastination. First, you must consider why you are procrastinating. Ask yourself: *Am I scared or ill-equipped to do the task? Am I afraid of failure?*

Acknowledging that you may not have all the skills or resources needed allows you to lower your expectation to get it right and takes the pressure off your shoulders. It also informs what you need to get started, effectively giving you your first course of action.

Then you can go to rules #3 and #6—creating a plan of attack and breaking down big tasks. This will ease some of the angst and keep you from feeling overwhelmed.

I also found that when I openly admitted to my peers and partners that I was struggling to start a particular assignment, they provided me with support and encouragement. That was all the spark I needed to get to work.

One last piece of advice that served me well: When struggling to stay focused and make progress, I would set a timer and take short breaks, and then go straight back to the task knowing that another break was just around the corner. If you haven't yet, try the Pomodoro technique: twenty-five-minute chunks of work separated by five-minute breaks. It got me out of trouble many times!

And as a rule, always **start your day by addressing the tasks you enjoy the least.** When you get to tick these boxes right away, it allows you to move through your day dread-free.

Think of it this way: The only acceptable time to procrastinate is when you put off procrastinating!

Rule #9: Focus on What's Important

I vividly remember the very first day my kids got into the car and buckled up all by themselves. I celebrated this major breakthrough and performed a little happy dance in my head. But while I was celebrating this major improvement in our logistics, I could feel the dread of the years flying by—a bittersweet moment.

Before you know it, kids go from needing a clean diaper to needing the car keys. While we are proud of the progress they make and applaud every milestone, we can't help feeling melancholic.

"You'll see, time goes by faster as you age."
Veronique to Agnès
Rio de Janeiro, Brazil

So mothers try to make the most of every moment knowing that the time they are given to pass down family values and build lasting family memories is fleeting. I have yet to hear a mom say, "I spent way too much time with my kids!" Somehow, mothers all come out on the other side of their kids' childhood feeling shortchanged.

For this reason, as a mom, I have always prioritized family time. But with our busy schedules, it was a rare commodity, so we tried to make it count. To ensure we had the opportunity to interact at least once a day, I asked that the entire family sit around the dinner table and that we all holster our electronics for the duration of our meal. And whenever possible, we played board games after dinner. We had spirited battles over Boggle, Clue, or Hedbanz—something I always looked forward to.

Despite meticulous meal planning and good intentions, I may have served breakfast for dinner at times. But in the bigger scheme of things, what was on our plates really did not matter. What did matter is that we spent time on what was important—having fun and interacting as a family.

The time spent talking, laughing, and simply creating memories for all of us was the most important moment of the day in my book. Kids grow up fast and time is too precious to waste. As my father-in-law always says, "Time is the one thing you can never get back!"

Following mothers' example, you can look at your list of to-dos and assess which ones truly add value and what matters most to achieving your long-term goals. Categorize each item and push down the ones that have little to no value. Doing so will make it easier for you to prioritize and manage your time well. Your long list may shrink down to a handful of items.

We are creatures of habit, and we settle into our routine because it is safe and comfortable. However, we sometimes do not see that we are wasting our time and not making any strides toward our long-term goals.

You can let life unfold and hope for the best, getting to the other side of sixty with lots of regrets. But when you manage your time well, you take control of your life. And as a leader, this should be your number-one priority if you hope to survive the onslaught of problems coming your way.

15

Where There's a Will, There's a Way

———

Every mom knows she should check her children's backpacks every so often to remove leftover food, trash, and the occasional important notification that should have been handed to parents months ago. This is how I came across a stash of thirty pencil grips in Jullian's backpack.

I wouldn't have thought much of it if it weren't for the fact that just the week before, Jullian had asked me for some money to buy a couple of pencil grips. For whatever reason, these were the fad of the moment, and every kid was hankering for their own assortment of grips.

Pencil grips came in a variety of colors and shapes. Some even had glitter. Kids placed the grips on their pencils to personalize them and, dare I say, make a statement about their brand. Even though they barely cost $1, I considered the expense frivolous and declined to give eight-year-old Jullian money to, um, establish his brand.

How in the world then did he come to possess so many grips? Apparently, I totally underestimated how resourceful my child could be when he really had his mind set on something. Here's how he proved to be a budding entrepreneur.

Jullian's best friend was a classmate named Lauren. Their friendship was unusual because, at that age, boys typically think girls have cooties, and girls think boys are gross. As a result, they tend to stick to being friends with kids of their own gender. But we had always encouraged Jullian to focus on other kids' qualities and values when selecting friends—not their cultural background, origin, race, and certainly not their gender.

As a result, Jullian and Lauren found they had much in common. They both liked Harry Potter, were avid readers, shared the same sense of humor, and simply enjoyed each other's company. To this day, I remember Lauren's mom, Kim, calling me to ask if Jullian would want to attend Lauren's birthday celebration at Universal Studios. When I promptly accepted, she told me there was a caveat—he would be the only guest.

I did not have a problem with that, so the two of them, chaperoned by Lauren's parents, had a blast at Universal that weekend. We supported and encouraged Jullian and Lauren's friendship. They were the exception to second graders' rule regarding friendship across the gender line.

Like all the other kids in their grade, Jullian and Lauren had their sights on getting their signature pencil grips. (Turns out that I wasn't the only parent that wasn't willing to fund the latest fad, after all.) So the two of them devised a plan that might pass for racketeering. Much like mobsters commit a crime against small businesses and then offer their "protection" against future problems, Jullian and Lauren created a demand, and then they provided the service.

Since their classmates were socializing according to gender— the boys on one side of the playground and the girls on another—

Jullian let the guys know that (wink-wink) he had heard the girls gossiping about them, and he knew for a fact that the girls were interested in getting more involved with the boys.

Meanwhile, Lauren did the same on her end. Suddenly, everybody was interested in knowing what the opposite side had to say, but few were brave enough to cross the threshold. So Jullian and Lauren graciously volunteered to act as couriers and pass messages back and forth. They would perform this favor for the affordable price of one pencil grip per message.

Voilà! Their business flourished.

Once I discovered the stash and had heard Jullian explain his innovative plan, half of me was alarmed while the other half beamed with pride. I wanted to know how they had come up with the idea.

Jullian explained that they both really wanted pencil grips—in other words, they were motivated by a shared goal. Since neither of them had the money to acquire the coveted goods, they had agreed they needed to encourage boys and girls to communicate so that they could offer to act as emissaries between both groups.

"Circumstances alter cases."
Olivia to Susan
McGregor, TX, USA

This communication channel offered the perfect outlet, albeit at a price.

I wasn't sure whether this side hustle of theirs could be an issue with the school. I decided that rather than shutting down their budding enterprise, I would let it play out. However, I set some rules of engagement. There would be no money involved. Should the school voice a concern, they had to be prepared to shut down all operations immediately. Finally, they had to update me periodically so I could monitor their activity from afar.

That's how I learned that the two of them had expanded their business. They charged one pencil grip for delivering a message and two grips if a response was to be brought back.

Jullian and Lauren's business became more complex when they also started delivering messages between the other grades of the lower school. Needless to say, they were kept busy running around the playground at recess, and their stockpile quickly grew.

> "Always make sure you do not have to rely on anyone to support yourself."
> Khadija to Mona
> Rabat, Morocco

In the end, they were past the point of caring about the grips. They just thoroughly enjoyed managing their business. Once the pencil grip fad fizzled out, so did their business. But by then, the boys and girls had finally become bold enough to communicate face-to-face.

Necessity is the mother of invention, they say, and Jullian and Lauren's enterprise surely supports this point.

Ultimately, giving them the freedom to pursue their initiative—though with some level of accountability—had given Jullian and Lauren the additional confidence to see their project through and expand on their initial gem of an idea.

In the end, their enterprise taught them that where there's a will, there's a way. Armed with resilience and perseverance, an open mind, creative thinking, and the willingness to combine ideas with individuals who have a different perspective (more on that in Chapter 19), anyone can shake up the system and find solutions.

> "The dogs may bark, but the caravan still moves on."
> Maria Manuela to Carlota
> Lisbon, Portugal

Often, all you need is just a new way to look at things and the freedom to try fresh options.

When you lead an organization, there is no such thing as smooth sailing. Roadblocks *will* arise, and your primary responsibility as a leader is to remove them.

Faced with problems or challenges, engage your team in problem-solving. If you trust them and they know you have their back, your team members will readily step up to the plate when presented with a challenge. When you appeal to people's ingenuity, it unlocks limitless creativity.

Look at what kids come up with. They let their imagination drive their thinking process without inhibitions. They do not restrict themselves to preconceived ideas or notions. Can you channel that can-do spirit as an adult? We all should. However, when growing up, we are too often taught to operate within certain parameters, to follow a predetermined process, to behave according to specific rules of engagement. This turns out to be a habit that is hard to break.

The same happens at work. We find comfort in routine and keep to our usual way of doing things. This inhibits our ability to think outside the box. Your role as a leader is to push the boundaries . . . or better yet, get rid of the box altogether. You can continue to facilitate the process with the following best practices.

Give Your Team Creative License

Encourage your team to seek creative solutions and try new things. Facilitate the process by allocating time for experimenting and expanding on ideas. **Make it safe to voice ideas** no matter how unconventional or seemingly outrageous.

If a leader is quick to shut down suggestions or ignore them altogether, no one will come back to the table with ideas. So be

mindful of how you react when someone brings up a suggestion—I certainly refrained from any initial comments when Jullian explained his little side hustle. Take a deep breath and count
to ten before you open your mouth. Then, ask open-ended questions, like "How does it work? . . . How did you come to this
solution? . . . What inspired this idea?"

Better yet, simply say, "Tell me more . . ."

Put Your Heads Together

Ken Blanchard famously said, "None of us is as smart as all of
us." Most ideas spring at the crossroad of a variety of perspectives,
skills, and backgrounds. Include anyone who shows interest—no
matter their title, role, or level of responsibilities. Involve people
from different departments or industries.

No one has a monopoly on creative thinking, and no one will
anytime soon. The answer to a problem often comes from unexpected places, improbable sources, and unassuming individuals.

**Hold regular group brainstorming and problem-solving
sessions** to assess the way you do things. This can deliver some
gems of ideas, not to mention the fact that it shows that you value
your team's input. Do not constrain them to think small. Let the
ideas grow. Some may seem impractical at first glance, but they
may spark the next idea and the next, leading to the solution you
have been looking for.

Be slow to judge or cast aside any suggestions. There will be
time later to come down to earth and think realistically. But initially, the sky's the limit!

Don't Look for *a* Solution. Look for *the Best* Solution

Don't settle for the easy fix. More often than not, the first incli-
nation will be to look for more resources. We need more money,

more people, more supplies, more space, more time . . . It's easy to cave in and fix whatever presents itself that way. There's just one slight problem: You may not have those resources available, or might choose to use those in other ways, just like I did by refusing to pay for Jullian's pencil grips.

Pressed by time, we also tend to settle for stop-gap solutions to take care of the symptoms, rather than looking for the root cause of a problem.

This can negatively affect your operation, your clients, and your employees—either further upstream or downstream. If you don't deal with the root of a problem, it may just morph into a different issue somewhere down the line. So make sure you think through all the implications of the solution or the creative idea you are about to put forth. Let all the players weigh in and consider how they will be affected.

By not settling for the easy or temporary solution, you push your team to consider all viable alternatives.

Get Some Fresh Air

Ever heard someone saying they had their best ideas while sitting at their office desk by their lonesome selves? Likely not. Ideas spring up in unexpected places—the outdoors, the beach, the shower . . .

Mothers know kids are most creative when playing outside because they let their imaginations run wild, untethered from structured playtime or screens. Mother Nature does wonders to the imagination, whether you're five or fifty-five. Dan and I do our best thinking while walking our dog and exploring the Colorado trails. So tell your team to *go take a hike!*

Let It Be Known that Failure Is an Option

French author André Gide once said, "Man cannot discover new oceans unless he has the courage to lose sight of the shore." In other words, there are no rewards without risks. And taking risks may cause you to get lost or, worse yet, lead to failure.

That is where most leaders or organizations draw a line in the sand. Time is money, we say. So we do not pursue opportunities, especially when it feels like the positive outcome seems distant and blurry. But *failure is good*.

It allows you to learn things you can build upon for the next experiment. It tests your resilience and pushes you to expand the boundaries of the creative process. Sometimes, it even leads to an unexpected outcome. John Pemberton was looking for a cure for headaches when one of his failed attempts became Coca-Cola!

So whether you're the one who failed or if it's someone on your team, take a step back. Look for what you can learn.

> "Do your best and then forgive yourself."
> Cherry to Kate
> Santa Fe, NM, USA

When it comes to overcoming challenges and finding creative solutions, there should be only one way to go. In Samuel Beckett's words, "Ever tried. Ever failed. No matter. Try again. Fail again. Fail better."

Start Small and Work Your Way Up

Pushed by your eagerness to problem-solve, you can get carried away by the prospect of implementing a new idea and possibly generating more revenue or solving a nagging issue. In doing so, you may be tempted to take on more than you and your team can handle.

Begin with the smallest executable steps, then grow from there. Jullian and Lauren started with a simple messaging service and later expanded to two-way communication. They initially focused on a small target clientele—delivering messages for their class during recess—and then broadened their scope to athletic teams and other grade levels, even deliveries before and after school.

A conservative approach mitigates the risks in case of failure and gives you the opportunity to fix issues if you hit a snag.

Be disciplined. Plan a conservative approach. Tweak at every turn and refine as you move through the implementation process. Scale when you are comfortable and confident with your new project or initiative.

Celebrate the Creative Process

Creativity is intelligence having fun. So, have fun! Enjoy the problem-solving process. Make it dynamic and entertaining.

People believe in their ideas, so give them a chance to defend them in a casual and risk-free format. Sometimes, employees keep their ideas under wraps until a big reveal because they're afraid of someone else taking credit for it. But they may also refrain from sharing an idea because they deem it unworthy.

If you create a fun environment, people tend to be less guarded and let go of their initial reticence. Even when their suggestions or ideas fail or you don't implement them, celebrate them! That's the surest way to keep them coming.

———

Encouraging problem-solving through creative thinking benefits a team or an organization in more ways than one. It promotes collaboration, boosts employee engagement, solves problems, and fosters an environment of trust where employees feel valued.

Leaders who invest in creative thinking attract exceptional talent—men and women who look for interesting challenges and forward-thinking organizations that won't settle for the status quo. When you push for creative thinking, it not only brings rewards in the form of innovative solutions, but it also sets your team on a path of constructive collaboration.

16
Plays Well with Others

—

Surviving the holidays is a feat, especially for moms. Starting mid-November, mothers are consumed with a seemingly never-ending to-do list as they plan menus, send Christmas cards, purchase and wrap gifts, send invitations for year-end celebrations, and decorate the house, among other things.

As if the flurry of activities isn't enough, Americans celebrate Thanksgiving less than a month before Christmas! When I moved to the US, I learned all the traditions this American holiday entailed and eventually became the designated Thanksgiving hostess.

The first time Dan's family came over for Thanksgiving, I opted not to make turkey and served them Moroccan couscous instead. *Quelle horreur!*

Though everyone hid their disappointment not to see a turkey and all the regular sides on the dinner table, they all graciously devoured the couscous. We had averted a diplomatic incident, but my culinary faux pas later became the source of many family jokes.

The next year, I learned how to stuff, baste, and roast a turkey. I also learned how to prepare all the traditional side dishes.

Believe me, there was no couscous in sight! And after what felt like a cooking marathon, the food disappeared in the blink of an eye. Everyone went home satiated and about three pounds heavier.

After a couple of years of solo performance as a host, it dawned on me that Thanksgiving was about bringing people together. What better way to do that than to bring everyone together *in the kitchen?* So I enlisted the help of Dan and the kids—and not just as mere sous chefs or cleanup crew. No! I wanted everyone to assume full responsibility for a dish and plan, prep, and cook it themselves. Why not?

Children often show a keen interest in helping, but we tend to relegate them to minor tasks for fear that their lack of competence may create more work for us. This erodes their self-worth and sends the message that they cannot possibly be good enough to take care of greater tasks.

I was determined to keep this from happening when it came to Thanksgiving. I have always assigned my kids chores, be it taking care of laundry or cleaning around the house. Surely, they could help with Thanksgiving dinner. So I laid out the rules. Whichever dish they chose, they were responsible for every step of the process, including helping with cleanup. I told them they needed to find a recipe, provide me with the shopping list, and be ready to execute on D-day. With that, Thanksgiving turned into a team sport.

Jullian (thirteen at the time) volunteered to make Brussel sprouts, Margot (ten) suggested mashed potatoes, and Tristan (seven) offered to make a holiday salad. Dan agreed to take care of the desserts. I was still the Grand Pooh-bah in charge of turkey and stuffing, but I was really grateful for the reinforcements.

On Thanksgiving Day, the kitchen was abuzz with activity as we jockeyed for counter space and oven time slots. It soon became obvious that without an agreement on how to proceed and general collaboration, there was no way we could get dinner ready by 5 p.m. when the rest of the family would show up.

We devised a plan, strategically divvying up the oven time. This would determine the rest of the logistics. Though the kids had all started the day focusing only on their own dish, before long, they were offering each other help and advice.

Margot offered to chop some of the salad ingredients for her younger brother and suggested a few tweaks to his recipe. Jullian monitored the oven to make sure we didn't overcook anything, and he helped out with basting the turkey. Tristan sampled dishes to share his opinion on seasoning, and he assisted with mashing the potatoes.

Everyone helped set and decorate the table. Then we all took care of cleaning the kitchen, which looked like a battlefield. Many hands make light work, so we managed to clear the piles of dirty dishes and wiped the counters clean before our guests arrived.

When we all sat around the table, I could tell how proud the kids were of their work and what we had accomplished *together*. Not only had the children fulfilled their personal assignments, but they had looked out for each other, spontaneously collaborated on some tasks, learned from their siblings, and in the process, they developed an appreciation for what they could achieve together.

That day, I was especially thankful for our family of five. Collaborating on hosting Thanksgiving resulted in an even better outcome and a more enjoyable experience for everyone involved.

The kids lavished compliments on each other's dishes and beamed with pride when the rest of the family praised them too. This became a yearly tradition, and the recipes became family favorites. As a mother, I had also found one more thing to be thankful for. My kids had just learned the important lesson that **success, much like meals, is more gratifying when it is shared.**

———

Through no fault of their own, young professionals often enter the workplace without a clear understanding of the mechanisms of effective collaboration. The school system often fosters competition and pits students against each other instead of encouraging them to collaborate. However, there are some obvious rules of engagement that can make working together second nature.

Know What Others Can Contribute

As a mother, I knew my kids' abilities and could make sure they were tackling tasks that matched their competence. I've said this and will say it again: Relationships are the heart of your business. When you know others, you understand what they bring to the table. And with that knowledge, you can leverage their abilities in reaching common goals.

Great leaders schedule social events where team members can discuss their areas of expertise. They encourage cross-functional job shadowing and assign mentors and partners on a rotating basis. All this **fosters peer-to-peer learning**.

When Margot was chopping ingredients for Tristan's salad, she showed him some basic knife handling skills I am sure were better received than if I had tried to teach him myself. In the workplace, when team members are learning and practicing their new skills with their peers, they can do so without the dread of being evaluated by their leader.

Often, all it takes for collaboration to sprout is a better understanding of everyone's role, responsibilities, skills, talent, challenges, and obligations. It gives you the confidence that you can rely on others.

Focus on the Overarching Goals of the Organization

Helping the team see the entire customer experience or the end product can help everyone get out of their silos and collaborate with teammates in other divisions.

When I was overseeing retail assortments for Epcot, we had just released the monorail toy set, and it was flying off the shelves. Because the monorail is a main show element of Epcot, most guests who flocked to our park hoped to get their hands on the coveted item.

A mere three days after its debut, I was told that the monorail was out of stock in the warehouse. How could this be? It appeared some not-so-well-intentioned leader at one of our other theme parks had ordered all the stock available and hoarded it, hoping to redirect revenue to his stores.

The individual did not bother to think of all the guests who would be disappointed not to find this toy set at Epcot. He had clearly lost sight of our shared mission to deliver the best guest experience possible, not to mention the fact that in the end, the revenue would end up in the same account, anyway. It took a robust phone conversation for him to catch on and get a grasp of Collaboration 101.

I made sure we shared the remaining inventory among all the appropriate locations, and I had the culprit's behavior documented. But the fragile trust in the other team's integrity and honesty had crumbled, and collaboration was at an all-time low. It was time for a reset. In the weeks that followed, I related this incident

"Did you remember to pack your manners?"
Maria to Adele
Jeffreys Bay, South Africa

to my team and beyond, making sure they understood that this

behavior was unacceptable and that we should all rise above this
kind of pettiness.

———

I'm sure you can substitute this example with one of your own.
Unfortunately, low and deceitful moves like these are not uncom-
mon, especially in large organizations. So if you're confronted
with a similar situation, don't linger. Remind everyone involved
of your shared goals and explain how this kind of behavior affects
the organization at large. Deal with the problem quickly, respond
decisively, and ensure it does not happen again.

Have a Clear Workflow

With five of us in the kitchen on Thanksgiving Day, we quickly
realized we had to plan our prepping and cooking time slots. A
well-defined process ensured that everyone knew when to show
up and when resources were available, be it oven or counter space.

It's OK for team members to work on a project at different
times as long as they complete their tasks by the deadline. A clear
workflow allows all team members to know when the team needs
their contribution. This helps them to manage their time better,
and when you don't need their input, they can attend to other
matters while the project moves along.

Make Collaboration Part of the Staff Review

Mothers know all too well that if you want to deter certain
behavior, you sanction it. If you want to promote another, you
reward it. You seek greater collaboration? Make it part of the
employee review process. Require your team to reach out across
the aisle and engage with peers. Assess and document how your

team members have successfully partnered and how often they have engaged with each other. Consider the following performance criteria.

Does this person welcome others' input?

Is this person non-judgmental and open-minded?

Does this person keep others informed?

Does this person support others and provide them with constructive feedback?

Does this person prioritize group efforts toward a common goal?

Does this person leverage the talents, skills, and abilities of others?

Does this person celebrate the achievements of others?

At Disney, the buying office product developers could comfortably monitor sales from afar, yet I found that their success was always directly proportional to their willingness to engage with the rest of the merchandise division. So I often encouraged them to join me for store walk-throughs.

On these walk-throughs, they could engage with the operations team, get to know each other personally, find common ground, and share their challenges and perspectives. By the end of the day, everyone was ready to support each other toward their shared goals.

They not only benefited from feedback and ideas from their partners, but they also gained a generous serving of goodwill.

Celebrate Wins

Measure and celebrate shared results. Then give public shout-outs to teams that successfully completed a project. **Celebrate challenges that were overcome *because* of collaboration.**

Ask your teams to share—or humbly brag—about collaborative efforts. There is nothing wrong with advertising the collective wins of the team. You can even provide tools so that team members can practice peer-to-peer recognition. When coworkers acknowledge others' contributions, they are more inclined to support each other in the future. It worked with my kids, and it works just as well with professionals.

Set the example by sharing the spotlight with deserving partners. It is important that leaders show that the success of others matters to them as much as their own. They should celebrate ideas, initiatives, and contributions from other areas of the organization and support their implementations, much like our family did in the kitchen.

When leaders reach out to people for input from different departments and if they regularly offer support to others, the rest of the team will follow suit and be supportive of one another. Gradually, it will become part of the culture of the organization.

Teams that regularly celebrate collaborative efforts reap greater benefits in times of crisis by banding together to overcome obstacles. They already know that they have each other's backs, communication flows easily, and they identify and solve problems sooner. Plus, less work gets duplicated, and everyone is on the same page because they are working toward the same goals.

When Collaboration Slows Down the Process

There may be rare occasions where collaboration slows down the process, especially in large organizations. These tend to be bureaucratic and may operate in a way that hampers the ability to roll out new projects rapidly due to so many departments being involved.

This can be easily alleviated by creating a small group of key players that have the dual responsibility of speaking on behalf of their different departments *and* have to keep everyone in the loop. This is how Disney developed MyMagic+. The project was designed to consolidate an array of functions ranging from credit card payments, room keys, park tickets, as well as reservations across the entire Walt Disney World property.

Considering the scope of MyMagic+, it was ironic that only five leaders formed the center hub of the project. Yet, this was the only way to quickly and efficiently push forward an initiative that involved the entire property.

Leaders must weigh the benefits of rushing along an initiative with a tight-knit group versus engaging with all the collaborators impacted by the project. Sometimes too many meetings, opinions, and people involved slow down the decision-making process. Sometimes speed is simply critical to a successful outcome.

Overall, there is no downside to collaboration. As the proverb goes, "If you want to go fast, go alone. If you want to go far, go together." Occasionally, you may encounter people who find it hard to get out of their silos. Others are downright reluctant and will take every opportunity to disagree with their peers and create discord. As a leader, you will have to manage and resolve such conflict—something mothers are all too familiar with.

> *"To be successful is to make satisfactory compromises with the inevitable."*
> Joy to Erin
> St. Petersburg, FL, USA

17
Can't You Just Get Along?

To their dismay, mothers often find themselves the designated referee to sibling rivalry. Even with a single child as their charge, they will eventually have to deal with conflict brought about by the teenage years. This is when a child's usually sunny personality becomes, shall we say . . . challenging.

Even if the first decade of the child's life was textbook perfect and a mom only occasionally had to exert power to get her child to cooperate, things change as soon as adolescence hits. She has to weather the storm of her teenager's hormonal changes and now faces passive-aggressive responses and confrontational behaviors.

Bette Davis famously said, "If you've never been hated by your child at least once, you have never been a parent." Moms may not always be fully prepared to deal with conflict but once again, they can't lay off their kids and there are no buy-back programs or returns.

And because they won't surrender parental responsibility to dads, teachers, coaches, or anyone else, for that matter, they have no other choice but to lay down the law.

As you may know from your childhood, conflict comes in many forms. There's the everyday nagging and bickering ranging from "He ate my cookies!" to "She keeps changing the channel." I've even heard a melodramatic, "He's breathing my air!"

Occasionally, conflict can turn to more consequential quarreling with assorted yelling, name-calling, and door-slamming. It may even end with one of the protagonists getting pushed around. In such instances, mothers typically reach for the classic threats: "Slam that door one more time and I *will* remove it!" or even "Watch your mouth or I'll get the bar of soap!" (Don't know about you, but I can still taste the soap.)

> "Never say unkind things to each other, even if you both know you're joking."
> Patricia to Michelle
> Rochester, NY, USA

Often, these theatrics happen behind the scenes with no adults in the room. It means that without you *witnessing the deed*, getting to the bottom of an argument is like peeling onions: It takes way too long and sooner or later, you are in tears. Somehow, mothers live to tell the tale. Here is mine.

It was 7:15 on a sunny Florida morning, and the kids and I were in the middle of our daily commute to school. Traffic slowed down to a crawl as we got closer to downtown Orlando, but we still had plenty of time to make it on time.

Margot and Tristan were debating the merit of some TV shows when Jullian asked them to keep it down so that he could study for his social studies test.

Margot snapped right back. "It's a bit late to do that!"

When Jullian hit back with a "Mind your own business," things unraveled.

Tristan sided with his sister, and the two of them ganged up against their older brother. The tone of the conversation rose, and the bickering turned into a full-blown argument.

I was past the point of trying to reason with them. Besides, I was trying to focus on driving. But the argument was dragging on and traffic didn't let up. My patience had run out. It was time to teach them a lesson.

I pulled over, pushed the button to open the minivan sliding door, and simply told the kids, "Get out."

We were in a residential neighborhood but still a little over a mile away from school, so they stared at me puzzled. "Why, Mom?!"

"Because I said so!"

Once they realized I meant business, they got out. I pushed the button to close the door and simply drove off.

To this day, I remember the look of shock on their faces. They probably wondered if I had lost my mind. Now, don't worry. I didn't abandon my kids. I just drove around the corner, parked the car, and waited a few minutes so I could regroup and get my emotions in check. Then I went back to where I had dropped them off.

By then, they had started walking toward school. They hadn't gotten far, though, so they were relieved to see me pull up. When I opened the door again, they got back into the van in total silence.

No one said a word. No one asked a question. Not one of them complained. The brief break had allowed them to let off steam and calm down. By that point, I am pretty sure they couldn't even remember what the argument was all about. I had diffused the situation—for a moment, at least.

"Remember, when I am dead, you will only have each other!"
Tosia to Marisza
Montréal, Canada

I knew there had to be a better way to get the kids to stop squabbling. So I devised a plan. I got a jar, better known as the "peace and love" jar. I reckoned calling it the "ceasefire jar" would have been more appropriate, but in the spirit of creating a positive environment, I settled on peace and love. Here's how it worked.

I took the kids' weekly allowance—just a few dollars—converted it to quarters, and put the total amount into the jar, which I kept on the kitchen counter. From then on, every time I heard whining, bickering, or quarreling, I removed a quarter from the jar. By the end of the week, I equally divided what was left between the kids.

The first couple of weeks, they were stunned to find that their allowance had all but evaporated. It didn't take too long for them to realize that there was a simple way to save their money—they simply had to change their behavior! The change didn't happen overnight, but I soon noticed a significant improvement. Eventually, peace was restored, and the house got a lot quieter.

Of course, they had the occasional argument but, for the most part, they bit their lips or removed themselves from the room to avoid potential tense confrontations—anything not to have me take money from the jar!

It seems they all agreed not to poke the bear. I couldn't help but chuckle when the tension rose, and I would hear one of them remind the others about the dreaded jar and the potential consequences should they choose to argue. Nothing works like a bit of peer pressure!

Along the way, I discovered the surprising upside to sibling rivalry. Thanks to the peace and love jar, my children were managing their conflict, they were mastering the art of ignoring each other's provocative behaviors, and they were resolving their differences. And they were doing this all on their own! In the process, they learned to negotiate and compromise.

I listened to them debating and reasoning with each other. I noticed that Tristan, being the youngest and often outwitted by his older siblings, would often get the short end of the stick. I pondered whether I should intervene, but before I could, Tristan had already learned to stand up for himself. It was only a matter of days until he became more assertive and made his voice heard.

I couldn't help but reflect that all these skills would serve them well through the years. Come to think of it, there is something to be said about the positive side of conflict!

———

As a leader, it would be preposterous to think you will be spared. Conflict is inevitable. You will run into the occasional discord due to differences in personalities, styles, agendas, and priorities. As much as you'd like to let your team members sort it out on their own, you must acknowledge it is happening and swiftly address it. Here is how.

Identify the Right Time and Place for Conflict Resolution

In most cases, rather than moving swiftly, it's wise to step away for a moment, just like I did when I dropped my kids at the curb and drove off to regroup. Mothers use time-outs not to punish but to give their kids—and themselves—the opportunity to calm down. Stepping away from a heated situation allows everyone time to get their emotions and their amygdala under control.

In the same way, sleeping things off can provide everyone with the opportunity to elevate their thinking and see the bigger picture. Give them some space so that they can regroup and think rationally again. This is why mothers' directive to "Go to your room" works so well.

Then, when you're ready, find a private, neutral location—preferably not your office—to address the matter with the stakeholders. Addressing issues in public is disrespectful. It will feed office gossip, and there's no need to drag others into the conflict and have them take sides.

And like in all difficult negotiations, you will often find that by bringing all the protagonists in the same room, you already have minimized the disagreement.

Let Them Have Their Say . . . and Listen

Before you jump to conclusions, have a meeting with those who seem to have been slighted. Listen to what they have to say. Consider that there may be extenuating circumstances that affect team members' performance or their emotional reactions.

As a leader, foster an environment where people are free to voice their concerns and dissenting opinions, provided it's done respectfully, of course. Whatever you do, make sure everyone feels safe to speak up.

Encourage everyone to take a big breath and express their disagreement. Make it clear that arguing doesn't serve any purpose other than possibly making people feel better by getting things off their chests.

On that note, Dan and I were recently part of an interesting experiment. A skilled moderator brought an audience of fifty to debate the most polarizing issues of our time: gun control, freedom of speech, and abortion rights. Needless to say, everyone was ready for a dogfight.

The format started with two volunteers from opposite ends of the opinion spectrum, each being given three minutes to explain their point of view. No one could interrupt.

Then the moderator summarized the points made on both ends, after which he opened the floor to the audience for questions and remarks. While everyone had been listening respectfully up to this point, we could not help but notice participants becoming more hostile, the comments being more caustic, and the tension rising. People became more vocal, more condescending, even aggressive.

The moderator was prepared for this to happen. Sensing that we were approaching the breaking point, he motioned to his assistant to blast some disco music. We were all required to dance. The sillier the dance moves, the better.

We all complied and, in the process, we released the tension that had been building up. After five minutes of sheer nuttiness, we were ready to tackle the next topic.

In the end, I am not sure anyone changed their positions on any issues. However, this exercise forced us to not only *hear* both points of view but also *listen* to the arguments that were presented, something that does not happen too often nowadays.

I believe we all went home with something to think about. I, for one, found it enlightening and learned a lot.

In conflict management, the challenge is to get both sides to not let emotions take over while actually listening to the arguments being made. You should require that everyone involved respectfully listen to each other's point of view. As a mom would say, "Wait for your turn to speak!"

If you can accomplish this and resist the temptation to mentally prepare your answer while others are speaking, it will start to move the needle in the right direction—even without the dancing.

Quit the Blame Game

Consider that some individuals try to boost their standings by deflecting responsibility and blaming others, much like a child would try to make a sibling look bad by saying, "It's her fault! She started it!"

It is one thing to point out others' mistakes when looking out for the well-being of the business, and another to put others down purposefully. Mothers do not encourage tattling, and neither should you. As I used to tell my kids, the only time tattling is acceptable is when it is meant to get someone *out of trouble*. As a leader, you would be wise to follow the same approach with your team.

In a professional environment, gossip and finger-pointing are more subtle than among kids, but such behaviors are still damaging. Instead, get to the root of the problem.

Be thorough in investigating the reasons for the frustration. Ask why the team members feel the way they do. You may unearth deeper issues related to your org chart, your processes, or personal matters.

Build on Common Ground

As the retail assortment manager for Epcot, my job required me to promote and facilitate collaboration between the retail operation team and the buying office. When business was great, the entire retail team praised each other. When business was tough, the *other* department would quickly become a scapegoat. If one retail location wasn't performing well, the operators were quick to point out the products that were out of stock or the prices that were deemed too high.

Meanwhile, the product developers at the buying office would blame the operators for either not staffing the stores adequately, not being attentive to the guests, or being too slow to restock the shelves.

My role often included making the parties on either side of a divide understand that no one could win at the expense of the other. We had a choice. We could either all win together, or we'd lose together.

Whether we won or lost would be determined by whether our guests exercised their buying power or not. That was the final yardstick by which we would measure all performances.

This scenario is not unusual. Companies often operate in silos. This leads to them failing to rally around a common purpose or collaborate. And when teams aren't working toward a common goal, unhealthy competition bubbles up. This leads to tempers flaring up as the stakes get higher. To find a solution, you'll have to identify what the common goal is, then focus on building upon that goal. As a team, **identify the outcome that everyone can agree upon**.

Be prepared, though. Every organization has team members— even entire departments—with divergent priorities. Do not let them lose sight of what you are trying to accomplish as a business: meeting your customers' needs and wants.

Those same customers couldn't care less about your internal conflicts or difference in priorities. Instead, they care about the outcome, the service, or the product you provide. They vote with their dollars. So when you're dealing with conflict, don't forget that the only goal is to serve your customers in such a way that everyone wins.

When you provide your team with a common objective, that goal must supersede individual tasks and responsibilities. In doing so, team members break out of their silos and see beyond the divergent priorities.

Explain Your Decision

Leaders must try to negotiate until every party involved is happy with a decision. However, there will be times when you won't be able to satisfy everyone. When that happens, take the time to explain the reasoning behind the decision—something slightly more challenging than declaring, "Because I am your mom, that's why!"

You may not be able to get people's agreement, but you must get their support. Providing clarity and explaining a decision-making process will ensure that they feel valued and respected, even if they are on the wrong end of the decision.

Along the way, you may have to identify some strategies to help those who are resisting conflict resolution. Help them see how every decision impacts not only them but your customers.

For my kids, their common goal was keeping the peace and love jar full. They were interested in making sure they'd receive their allowance.

So, what's in your team's jar?

———

One of the worst things that can happen is for leaders to evade conflict and dodge confronting issues. The longer you wait, the higher the odds that resentment will fester. And take my word—it *will* contaminate the team. People will gossip, take sides, and denigrate others. There will be bitterness or even hostility among the protagonists. So don't delay your answer.

If anything, conflict presents opportunities. As a leader, you will benefit from engaging with dissidents. They are not just plain agitators or insurgents; they have a point of view or a reason that is valuable no matter what, so open your mind and listen intently.

There is always a nugget of pertinent insight into different perspectives and divergent opinions. You don't have to agree, but you must pay attention anyhow.

When you confront the issues head-on, encourage discussion and negotiation, and focus on the common goals, you prevent the environment from becoming toxic and show your team that disagreement can, in fact, have a positive outcome.

And when you come out on the other side you may be bruised, but the wiser for it. Managing conflict successfully is the ultimate litmus test of a healthy culture . . . and a healthy family.

> *"We are all ignorant, each of us on a different subject."*
> Marcela to Anna
> Mexico City, Mexico

18

Navigating the Rapids

———

I n the summer of 2006, the kids and I were vacationing in France. Always on the lookout for a bit of adventure, I took my kids and my two nieces on a canoe outing down a nearby river. At five, Tristan was the youngest of them all. The oldest of the group was fourteen.

The river was easy to navigate and did not have any steep gradients, so I figured we'd all have a blast. With five kids in tow, off we went on a sunny afternoon. Margot, Elise, and Sophie wanted to ride in one canoe, and the boys and I were in another, Tristan safely sandwiched between Jullian and me.

About two hours into what was to be a four-hour trip, I noticed the river narrowed, causing the water to rush through the bottleneck. The river seemed to be a lot deeper in that area.

The boys and I skirted the edge of the bottleneck so we could avoid the full force of the current, but the girls' canoe hit a fallen tree hidden under the water, spun sideways, and flipped over. Elise and Sophie immediately popped back up, but Margot was nowhere in sight.

I feared that her life jacket had gotten tangled in the branches, making it impossible for her to surface. I needed to act quickly! My instinct kicked in and I dove into the water to rescue my daughter. But I was a good six feet downstream from the upside-down canoe stuck to the tree, and the force of the current prevented me from reaching it. It felt like an absolute nightmare!

I suddenly realized what I needed to do. I got out of the water, ran up the bank a bit, and dove back into the river so the current would take me to where my daughter was stuck. Those few seconds felt like an eternity.

Fortunately, the current slammed me right into the canoe, dislodging it. With that, Margot emerged, and I pulled her to the bank where we caught our breath. The moment Margot could breathe normally again, she burst into tears. I was deeply thankful for these tears. That she was crying was good; it meant she was breathing.

Next, I checked on the rest of the crew, only to find that Tristan was alone in our canoe—Jullian had jumped in after me to help save his sister—and was floating downstream. Fortunately, Elise and Sophie were running along the bank, chasing him. They soon caught up with the canoe as the river widened and the current considerably slowed down.

Once we were all safely back together, we assessed the damage. We had lost two paddles and a camera, plus a few pieces of clothing that were floating downstream. But we were all alive, and that's all that mattered!

After comforting the kids—Margot had settled down by now—I told them we'd have to get back into the canoes so we could reach the spot where someone from the rental company would pick us up. Understandably, the children were reluctant to continue, but we had no other option.

My goal was to get all six of us home safely. I assured the kids we would proceed carefully, and if I saw another bottleneck, we'd get out and pull the canoes along the bank till the water slowed down again.

Margot mustered the courage to get back into the canoe, and the others followed. I tried to make light conversation as we started down the river, but the edginess was palpable, and the normally chatty cousins were quiet. When we finally reached the meeting point, relieved to be on dry ground, I congratulated the kids for their fortitude and resilience.

When Dan called from the US that evening to hear about our canoe trip, the magnitude of the day's events finally hit me. I broke down crying as I realized how badly this could have ended.

To this day, I don't know how I managed to think clearly enough to extract Margot from the river. I would imagine it was sheer motherly instinct.

I'm infinitely fortunate not to have faced similar circumstances on too many occasions, but the events of that summer day gave me an understanding of what it takes to manage through a crisis.

———

Leadership is hard enough when things are running well, but in times of crisis is when true leaders show what they're made of. This is when hopeful eyes turn toward the top of the org chart and look for a solution. There are a few critical steps that leaders must take.

Assess the Situation

As you and your organization encounter unforeseen crises, you cannot dodge these responsibilities or appear uncertain. You need to act. But before you can act, you must assess the situation and decide whether to move quickly or gather more facts.

If the crisis requires immediate action, act swiftly. But if you have time, take a moment to pause, especially if the decisions you're about to make might have crucial consequences. Carefully consider the big picture and long-term implications before you make any decisions.

> "A cautious woman is as valu-able as two of them."
> Libertad to Jessica
> Cabimas, Venezuela

Don't hesitate to get input, but be mindful of analysis paralysis, where fact-finding takes up so much time that it renders the decision-making even more challenging. Meanwhile, your team may be getting more anxious, the problem becomes even more overwhelming, and anticipatory stress clouds everyone's judgment.

The longer the crisis remains unresolved, the more damage to your credibility. So do what you can to reestablish a level of normalcy.

Don't Let Emotions Get in the Way

When Margot disappeared under the water, I rightfully feared for her life and had an intense emotional reaction. Unfortunately, these kinds of **emotions cloud your judgment, making it hard to think clearly and make rational decisions.** (This is known as the amygdala hijack.)

In a crisis, do whatever it takes to get your emotions under control so you can focus on the most pressing matters. It's OK to feel some emotions, but these should not control you. Instead, take a big breath and use the adrenaline rush to focus your entire attention and energy on the matter at hand.

Focus on What Matters Most

Ask yourself, *What matters most?* Once you know the answer, focus on that. Now isn't the time to chase multiple outcomes or look for a perfect solution.

On 9/11, as US landmarks were being attacked, we immediately evacuated all Disney parks. Keeping visitors out of harm's way was the sole priority. Not for a moment did Disney consider lost revenue or possible disgruntled guests. The parks remained closed until it was deemed safe to reopen.

Sometimes you may deal with a dilemma where there are no suitable solutions. Consider what you may have to sacrifice, again going back to what is most important. You may have to go with what your gut tells you.

Whatever you do, act. The worst that can happen is inaction and lack of decisiveness. You don't want to look back wishing you had done something . . . *anything!*

Restore Confidence

Keep in mind that your team's emotions are running high too. Only if you can stay calm will you be able to defuse the tension among your staff and allow them to think rationally. To **ease team members' anxiety, keep your composure.** Emotions are contagious, so choose to spread calm rather than anxiety.

During our canoeing crisis, I was keenly aware of the fact that the kids were looking for how I'd act as we resumed our trip. I could not let them see how anxious I was! My confidence had been shaken, but the last thing the kids needed was some nervous wreck of a mother leading the way.

Talk to Your People

In my experience, communication breakdowns compound crisis situations. Yet this is when you need to be the most diligent about communicating. When things seem to be falling apart is when you need to be transparent about your decisions and explain why you are doing what you're doing. If you don't communicate, your team may jump to conclusions and make assumptions that can make matters worse. So **communicate even more than you normally do.**

Not only will it reassure the team that the situation is being addressed and under control; it will also prevent the situation from getting out of hand. Even if you don't have all the facts or all the answers, tell them what you *do* know. *Some* communication is better than none.

Address the Cause Later

There will come a time to assess the why of the crisis. But this should only happen once the dust has settled, and you can rationally examine the problem and get to the root cause.

As for our canoeing fiasco, I blamed myself for going on such a trip with five kids and no other adult to help. Of course, I also explained to the canoe rental company what had happened so they could warn future clients and possibly even remove the hidden tree—quite literally the root cause of our crisis.

———

In the end, there are always lessons to be learned from these experiences. Dealing with crisis situations reveals a lot about character and how much you can handle.

Some people crumble under the weight of decisions and look to others. Some freeze and cannot function at all. Some rise to the challenge. Adrenaline, if channeled properly, allows you to do things you would otherwise not be capable of. It can boost your strength, stimulate your courage, heighten your reflexes, raise your ability to focus, and increase your brain power.

As such, dealing with a crisis forges character. It allows you to continue to grow in knowledge, skills, and valuable experience—something that you may find hard to appreciate while in the middle of the storm.

Looking back, you will eventually come to realize how much you have learned while confronted with crises. And when you're a leader, you find out that there's so much you actually *don't* know, and so much you have yet to learn. Which brings us to the need for continuous self-improvement.

19
Just Keep Learning

———

September 2, 1995 is a day etched in my memory as the start of a profound new phase of personal development. It's the day Jullian was born.

The moment the nurse placed my son in my arms, the magnitude of the responsibility of motherhood hit me. I knew that from that day forth, I would never stop learning. Being responsible for another human being changes your perspective and causes you to reconsider how you approach life in general.

Suddenly, there was an ever-growing list of new skills to acquire and a plethora of decisions to be weighed, none of which came easy. And just when you think you know what you're doing and can copy and paste your knowledge with the next child, you learn that no two kids are the same.

As I have mentioned, I was woefully unprepared to raise children. I had never taken care of a newborn, much less changed a diaper or given a baby a bottle. I had a bit of practice with toddlers from my experience as an au pair in London, but that essentially revolved around effective ways to keep them fed and entertained.

I did not know that at night, babies sometimes cry not because they are hungry but because they need to be comforted.

I did not know it was best to purchase half a dozen pacifiers just in case, and that you should have two of your child's favorite bears.

I knew absolutely nothing about dealing with sibling rivalry other than from my experience with my sister.

I did not know I could hide and serve veggies in the form of smoothies and that lint rollers are great to pick up glitter.

> *"Always buy two of everything you need, just in case."*
> Carol to Marcy
> New York, NY, USA

I also did not know that cold water can put an end to a tantrum.

I did not know the benefits of an established routine and the art of reverse psychology.

I did not know that when a sibling comes along, toddlers act out to get attention when they feel slighted or ignored.

I did not know the power of repetition and the magic of positive reinforcement.

I did not know that you could make multiplication tables fun to learn by teaching them while playing Twister, or that you could motivate your child to read basic words by hiding flashcards around the house and playing Hot or Cold.

I was clueless as to the psychology and diplomacy required to deal with the challenges of raising a teenager.

I did not know how to read the signs of overstimulation, upcoming temper tantrums, and allergic reactions.

You get the idea. This list is never-ending.

So I read books about parenting, consulted with friends and relatives, sought advice from professionals, and even turned to Google for information and best practices. But because each kid is unique, I quickly realized that I would have to learn most of it on the job.

Children all respond to different things, so I had to decide how to proceed, put my strategy to the test, and then tweak, adapt, or adopt an entirely different approach.

There is no 100% foolproof parenting playbook. So just like all the other moms, I just had to figure it out. I had to learn while *doing*.

This is why being a mom is hard, perplexing, and humbling. Learning on the job quickly lets you see your limitations and your shortcomings. Children can throw all kinds of curve balls that lay bare your flaws and imperfections. And this happens in plain sight.

Should you forget, kids also have an innate talent to jog your memory and remind you that you don't know it all. In fact, by the time they are teenagers, they make it clear that, in their opinion, you don't know a thing!

To be a mother and love a child is like a strenuous workout—it can hurt in places you didn't know existed, especially your ego and your confidence. So as kids grow and change, so do you. You learn better ways to prepare children for the challenges they face, even the ones you never had to deal with yourself. You learn new skills and different approaches.

Mothers remain laser-focused on raising the most perfect children. They assess and analyze their own performance and are often their own worst critic, holding themselves to high standards. They discover their limitations, lay bare their vulnerability, and try to improve as they go. They remain committed to being the best mom they can be, knowing that they never, never stop learning.

"Bloom where you're planted."
Dolly to Susan
Bonn, Germany

———

Have you ever tried to list all the qualities and behaviors of great leaders? If so, you're probably still working on that list. It's never-ending and quite overwhelming. There's not one leader from the past, present, or future who'd ever be able to check the boxes of all those qualities.

But one common characteristic of such leaders is that they are avid learners, and, just like mothers do, they understand that learning never ends. So they keep sharpening their skills and expanding their knowledge.

William Pollard eloquently said, "The arrogance of success is to think that what you did yesterday will be sufficient for tomorrow."

I'd like to add to that, "What you *knew* yesterday will not be enough for tomorrow." I learned that the hard way while discovering the distinct personalities and needs of each of my children.

In business, things change way too fast and become more complex by the day. If you think you have all the knowledge you need, think again. You can always improve.

If you've read this far, I assume you're interested in being a better leader. And to make this happen, you need to look at your calendar and dedicate time to the following.

Learn Anytime and Anywhere

To do so, read widely, attend lectures, listen to TED Talks, join LinkedIn Learning, and engage with your peers, experts, or a mentor. Join a mastermind. Better yet, hire a coach who can guide you in identifying goals for yourself. Not only can that person provide you with direction and encouragement, but this will provide you with the added commitment to self-improvement, as you will be accountable to someone else who has given you time and support.

You don't have to wait for a poor performance review, a heart-to-heart with your own leader, or for your shortcomings to become glaring to pull out the stops and embrace learning. **The best thing you can do for yourself, your family, and your team is to do all you can do to grow** so you can better face life's trials and tribulations.

Learn from Your Mistakes

Imagine having just completed a project or a complicated task. You may be eager to celebrate with a glass of champagne or simply move on to the next project. Not so fast! First, you need to take a critical look at what you've just completed.

Practice your own postmortem review. Consider what you could have done better. Ask yourself, *If I were to do this again, would I do it the same way? What worked? What didn't?*

Learn from your challenges, mistakes, and failures. A mistake is only tragic when you fail to draw from its lessons. Make notes of what you have learned and apply the lessons to your next project.

"If only I were twenty years old and knew what I know now . . ."
Anna to Valerie
Lyon, France

If you think this is a waste of time, consider the alternative—making the same mistakes over and over again.

Learn from Your Team

When pressured to deliver results, you can easily slip into the habit of just executing what you deem is the best course of action without stopping to involve your team. You fail to encourage questions or challenges to your line of thinking.

At times, leaders even unintentionally direct their questions toward a desired answer by using closed-ended questions which do not invite the use of analytical or critical skills. This limits the range of answers, even if involuntarily.

On the other hand, the use of open-ended high-level questions opens the door to important insights and generates more viable options.

Such is the difference between asking, "What are the steps of our client registration process that need to be improved upon?" and "How would you design an improved client registration process?" The former is restrictive in its scope. The latter invites more input and a wider range of answers.

In a similar fashion, have you ever caught yourself asking, "Don't you think we should . . .?"

This isn't an actual question. You're simply making a suggestion, and your team might feel uncomfortable disagreeing with you when presented this way.

When asking for input from your team, take a deep breath and get comfortable with a bit of silence. Let your question sink in. Some of your team members may need a moment to organize their thoughts, formulate an answer, or come up with a suggestion. You may have been mulling a problem for a while, but it may be the first time they've ever heard it.

Continue with open-ended follow-up questions to allow more input and show that you truly are interested in learning from them. And then, speak last when sharing your point of view.

Create Self-Development Goals

Self-development is a long-term investment that does not yield immediate results. So we postpone it, claiming we'll get to it when we have time and energy or when there aren't fires to put out. That day will never come.

Other priorities will fill your schedule until you intentionally set aside time for growth, just like you might set aside time to go to the gym.

To ensure you prioritize self-development, formalize it for your team and yourself. Require that everyone sets goals to develop skills, competencies, and knowledge. Then hold yourself and the team accountable by adding it to performance reviews. This will provide the incentive to prioritize this crucial element of growth.

———

Life keeps teaching and we never stop learning. But while leaders might direct self-development at areas of expertise that align with their role and responsibilities, there is something to be said about stretching one's mind by venturing into new areas and experimenting. This is why great leaders benefit from having a curious nature.

20

Where Do Babies Come From?

—▬—

When we first took the kids to France, we'd drive cross-country at the speed of about 100 questions an hour. "Why are the buildings so old? . . . Why do French people drive so fast? . . . Who decided snails were food? . . . Do they really wear berets?" Of course, there was also the old staple, "Are we there yet?"

Once we finally reached our destination, the questions kept coming. "How many times a week do they eat frog legs? . . . Do they drink wine for breakfast? . . . Why is she wearing a necklace on her teeth?" (That one came from Margot seeing a girl with braces).

Kids aren't shy about their ignorance. Instead, they let their natural sense of inquiry surface. They want to know why people behave the way they do, how things work, what the future holds . . . and where babies come from. They're curious about everything life has to offer.

Granted, their non-stop stream of questions can be exhausting at times. Plus, moms don't always have the answers. If I ever found myself in this situation, my go-to answer was, "What do you think?"

This question invites children to use their critical thinking and come up with a plausible answer of their own, not to mention that it elicits countless entertaining gems straight out of their innocent mouths.

Once, while watching a space shuttle launch—a benefit of living in Florida—seven-year-old Jullian wondered out loud how NASA fixes the space shuttle if a problem emerges after take-off. Before anyone could answer, Margot (then four) confidently quipped, "With tape!"

Unfortunately, this sense of innocence, wonder, and curiosity wane as kids become adults. Why? Because we often learn at school that there's just one right answer, that we have to color within the lines, that we have to follow the rules and not waste time investigating solutions drawn from our imagination. This leaves little space for free-form expression, curiosity, and experimentation.

Questions are expected to fit within the boundaries of the curriculum, and schools do not encourage kids to think outside the box, effectively stifling curiosity and creativity.

I have always been one to encourage my kids to try things out. Not that I always applauded their experiments, especially the time they stuck a piece of gum on the outside of a plane while we were boarding just to see if it'd still be there upon landing! (For the record, it was. But it had turned into a two-foot-long sticky mess!)

Usually, though, I would just observe them having fun being their curious selves. For example, when she was eight, Margot and her friend Tara asked if they could make a "Tar-Got" salad. Curious about what they'd come up with, I gave them the green light to forage through the fridge and pantry.

I watched from afar as they carefully chopped and combined greens, carrots, and cucumbers. (So far, so good.) Then they added a cup of sliced strawberries (not my taste, but whatever). When it came to their dressing, though, I was horrified to see them carefully pour honey and yogurt over their salad, then add ground turmeric and a generous pinch of cayenne pepper for good measure. Then came the finishing touch: a spoonful of garlic powder topped with—wait for it—some chocolate fudge syrup. Just the thought of the combination of flavors is enough to make me gag.

I watched them dish up their Tar-Got salads and sit down ready to enjoy their creation. Sure enough, they ate every bite and proudly announced that this was indeed the best salad that they had ever tasted! For fear of being offered a serving, I chose not to argue with them.

I knew that beyond the fun of cooking together, the girls had gotten **the satisfaction of creating something without guidance.** I had to overcome the temptation to provide instructions or dictate what the outcome should look or taste like. Instead, I got out of the way, allowed them to follow their inquisitive minds, and let the learning unfold.

To this day, neither Margot nor Tara will forget that combining garlic, chocolate syrup, honey, and cayenne pepper is a recipe for disaster . . . even if they'll never admit it!

———

People are naturally curious, especially when confronted with new things, people, or surroundings. They never quite outgrow their inner six-year-old selves. They get energized and invigorated when given the chance to gain new knowledge that piques their curiosity.

When given the freedom to experiment, people will not only pay closer attention to the experience but also process the lessons more effectively—much like kids do when they can explore on their own. They will use their critical thinking, apply more effort, and reach better outcomes.

As a leader, you will benefit from encouraging your team to inquire, to experiment, and to generally follow the trail of their curiosity. Here are a few suggestions.

Cultivate Curiosity

When you're looking at developing new products or services, let your team "play in the kitchen," if you will, and create their own "salad." They will learn in the process and so will you.

There are calculated risks that you *can* and *should* take for the sake of learning. Foster an environment where you reward curiosity regardless of the outcome. Dedicate some resources so that you and your team can investigate new areas and pursue interests even unrelated to your activity.

Require that your team members figure out what they want to know, and then set them free to seek answers. This will further fuel their sense of autonomy and develop their ability to work independently. Given the ability to cultivate personal interests provides individuals with intellectual stimulation and fulfillment that will improve retention in your organization.

So why not start a team meeting by asking, "What have you learned lately that you can share with the group?" You will find the answers may range from trivial to truly informative.

Encourage Inquisitiveness

Leaders must help their teams to overcome inhibitors like assumptions and fear. So encourage your team members to ask odd questions and make suggestions—even if considered outlandish. Some questions will expose the truth and will lead to learning.

Others will challenge your thinking, which will help you grow as a person and as a leader.

In a business environment, team members often refrain from being curious and stick to asking safe questions—ones that will not compromise their standing in the organization or the established ways of thinking. Here's a hint: **If your team members aren't asking tough questions, it doesn't mean they don't have any.** It likely means they're too scared to ask them or know you won't listen.

Make it clear that you welcome challenging or seemingly odd questions. You can even consider assigning someone on your team to be the "inquisitor extraordinaire" for the day, someone who will push back on established thinking, venture into new territory, or ask out loud the pesky question on everyone's minds, the likes of, "What would happen if we were to do this . . .?"

Set an example by probing your team. "What do you think? . . . What's our best option here? . . . What would you do if you were in my shoes? . . . Is there something I'm missing or not thinking about? . . . How is this a problem? . . . What are some unconventional options? . . . Any crazy ideas which we should entertain?"

Host a Hack Day

Letting people experiment will not happen unless you provide a time and space for it. So if you can, schedule a day where the entire team can work on whatever strikes their fancy and their curiosity, as long as it is not part of their daily tasks.

It's a great opportunity to explore some new fields, activities, or even new technology. Let people work in groups or independently on the activities of their choosing. This will provide a break from the routine and may create opportunities for team members to interact with people from areas of the organization they rarely work with.

Be a Curious Leader

Curiosity is contagious, so you can fuel your team's curiosity by setting an example. Show interest in learning new skills. Ask powerful questions that will spark reflection and compel you to challenge the established way of doing things.

I found I could use the same questions I had used to prompt my children. "Why is this done this way? . . . How will this work? . . . What would happen if . . .?" And then I'd join them in finding the answers.

As a mom, I faced an onslaught of questions to which I didn't always have an answer. I could try to deflect with a quick, "That's just the way it is!" But kids are relentless with their questions. So I found that the best way to ignite curiosity not only with my kids but also with my team is to say, "Let's find out!"

————

Kids can see things objectively because they have no past references, so they aren't tethered by bias or preconceived ideas. (By the way, I agree with Margot, "necklace on her teeth" is a much more fun way to describe braces!). They let their curiosity drive their questioning, forcing their moms to come up with creative answers at times.

You and your team can benefit in the same way if only you will unlearn what you know, take a fresh look at how you operate, and consider unique approaches.

In the end, you will find that the thirst for knowledge grows exponentially. The more you know, the more you know how much you *don't* know. And this leads to the realization that the richer and more diverse the environment you operate in, the greater the lessons.

21

What a Wonderful World

———

Just four weeks after Jullian started kindergarten, the school invited us to an open house for parents. Glued to the back of each chair in the class was a self-portrait of each kid. So when we entered the classroom, there were twenty little hand-drawn faces staring at us.

Dan and I scanned the rows, searching for even the smallest detail that would give us a clue as to which seat belonged to our son. Try as we may, we simply couldn't identify Jullian's portrait. The teacher came to help, pointing us toward a drawing of a little brown face.

Turned out Jullian had drawn himself in the same color as his best friend, Kierin. It didn't matter that Kierin was of Indian descent. Dan and I cracked up laughing, much to the relief of the teacher. In fact, we couldn't be more thrilled that our son was oblivious to the fact that his skin color was, in fact, different from that of his best buddy.

This incident confirmed our view that kids are not born being prejudiced—they are *taught* to be prejudiced. Kids are blind to differences in skin color until they are taught differently by watching how people around them act and listening to what people say. And bit by bit, their worldview is shaped by what they've seen and heard, and they adopt those beliefs and mimic those behaviors.

This underscores the importance of moms modeling the appropriate behaviors by respecting and embracing diversity. They must be mindful of everything they do and say as teaching kids the value of diversity comes with many pitfalls and many challenges. And it goes far beyond diversity of race and skin color.

The summer of 2001 was the first year I took my children to Europe by myself. I had left my job at Disney to dedicate myself to raising my children for a while, so my kids and I finally had time to visit family in France.

As I had mentioned, the kids would ask a ton of questions on these trips, and their first visit to my home country was no exception. One day, the kids and I headed to the grocery store.

We parked our car and went to get a shopping cart. At most stores in France, they chain the carts together, and shoppers must insert a Euro coin to dislodge a cart. Once you return it and click the lock back in place, you get your coin back. You often find panhandlers strategically waiting nearby, knowing that shoppers are more susceptible to hand over the change they have in their hands.

So as we went to get our cart and headed toward the store entrance, seven-year-old Jullian asked, "Mom, what are these people doing?" I explained they were most likely homeless and in need of money to buy food.

Jullian was quiet as he mulled over my answer until he finally said, "We don't have people like that in America."

I was stunned. How could my children be so oblivious to the hardship that some face in the US? And then it dawned on me: We lived in a nice residential area close to Walt Disney World, where the magic extended to the local stores and facilities. My kids attended a first-rate school with children from affluent families, and we vacationed in France! They had simply never encountered poverty.

I was mortified. This immediately raised the question, *How much more were they unaware of?* This was not how Dan and I had intended to raise our kids. We were both aware of the diversity of our world, be it in terms of race, ethnicity, religious beliefs, sexual orientation, or living standards. Not only did we respect everyone, but we valued diversity, and we certainly hoped to raise our kids to behave and think the same way.

This experience opened my eyes to the need of being purposeful in imparting values such as embracing diversity. But first, I had to confront my own lack of awareness.

I remember discussing discrimination with Jamiko, the mother of one of Margot's schoolmates. Jamiko's family was African American. When I told her I had never witnessed any form of discrimination at the kids' school, Jamiko gently retorted, "Of course not! You're white."

So lesson one: **Just because you don't *see* or experience it doesn't mean it does not *exist*.**

Many years ago, just before Christmas, I witnessed a young African American teenager walking around our neighborhood. My first thought was with it being the Christmas season, there would be lots of parcels at people's front doors, and I wondered if the young man could be looking to steal some packages.

That's when it hit me—I wouldn't have made the same assumption had he been white. My first instinct had been to assume the worst simply because *he looked like he did not belong!*

I know I'm not alone. I believe we all make similar assumptions.

Some years later, I got to know Frances, an older homeless lady who was living on the streets in downtown Orlando. I spoke to her on several occasions and related our conversations to my family at dinner. I mentioned how surprised I had been to find her quite erudite and well-spoken.

No sooner had the words crossed my lips than I realized I was once again being narrow-minded. I had assumed that because Frances was poor and homeless, it had to mean that she was uneducated.

And these are just a couple of examples that I am aware of! I wonder how many times I have lacked the self-awareness to even notice what I was saying or thinking. I realize that working on identifying my biases is not enough, but it's a start.

That's lesson two: **We *all* have deep-rooted unconscious biases that cloud our judgment.**

It takes time and awareness to work on this, and I still consider myself a work in progress—as most of us should. But I'm committed to addressing the topic with my kids, my family, and my friends so I can develop the self-awareness required to acknowledge biases and encourage others to do the same.

I have also committed to seeking as many diverse experiences as possible for me and my kids. For example, we sent our three children to a Jewish Community Center (JCC) for preschool. Not being Jewish, this was a great learning experience for our entire family.

I had lots of questions and didn't want to make a faux pas, so my dear friend Marcy became my adviser on all things Jewish. That is how my kids and I learned about kosher food, Rosh Hashanah, Purim, Sukkot, Yom Kippur, and the many rituals of the Jewish religion. We often attended Shabbat and bar and bat mitzvahs, and we made lifelong friends in the process.

When we traveled, we opted not to stick to the usual tourist spots. We used local buses and sought out-of-the-way accommodations. On a trip to South Africa, we even stayed in Soweto and drank homemade beer at a local *shebeen,* a makeshift bar in the middle of a shanty town.

We have jumped at every opportunity to host people of all nationalities, cultures, and races at our home, and in doing so, forged incredible friendships. Every time we opened our doors to someone who was different from us, we became a little more knowledgeable about their experience and the world we all share.

As a result, I believe my children have done a far better job of embracing differences than I have, simply for the fact that we have exposed them early on to the gift of diversity and ensured it is omnipresent in our everyday lives. We can fear diversity, ignore it, or embrace it. Our family has chosen the latter, and I can honestly say we are the richer for it.

As a mom, I have learned to talk about diversity with my children, to highlight what people of different backgrounds share in common, to encourage them to meet people from all walks of life—even if it sometimes gets them out of their comfort zone—and to discuss what differences can teach us.

> "So many places to go, so little time!"
> Isabelle to Elise
> La Bâtie-Rolland, France

That's the third and final lesson: **Be purposeful about discussing, seeking, welcoming, and including diversity in your life.**

———

Look around your organization. If you all look the same, you have a problem. You have the same gender, age, and race, and as a result, you're more than likely looking at things from the same lens, drawing similar conclusions based on your similar backgrounds. You are missing out.

It's easy to gravitate toward people who are like us. It's comfortable and feels safe. Put me in charge of recruiting and if I'm not purposeful about diversity, I will primarily hire middle-aged women who speak with a French accent. That is called an affinity bias. Here is how you can prevent this from happening in your workplace.

Assess Your Selection Process

If you want to bring more diversity to your team, start by considering where you recruit. While you should always hire the best person, ensure that you **have a diverse pool of candidates**. How do you do that? Look for future new hires in a variety of places.

If you have any team members from minority groups on staff, ask them to refer some candidates. And to encourage minority applicants, showcase the diverse culture of your team, be it on your website or by inviting minority team members to take part in the selection process.

Use assessment tools to bring an objective methodology to your recruitment process and remove any discriminatory practices. And besides looking at whether a candidate fits your company culture, consider candidates who will *add* to the diverse wealth of your team, candidates who bring unique experiences, perspectives, and talents to the table.

Broadcast Your Values

There should be no ambivalence about where you stand on diversity. Be very clear about the fact that you value and respect everyone in your organization.

Much like a mother sets the example for her kids, leaders must be crystal clear about what is acceptable and what isn't. This starts with hiring candidates who align with your beliefs. Remember that prejudices are deeply rooted, and there is little chance you will change someone when their view differs widely from your own. The last thing you need is to hire someone who does not share your positions. If you are clear about where you stand, people who disagree with you will self-select out.

Consider Your Org Chart

We too often see a lonely token woman or person of color somewhere in a corner of the org chart. Consider the makeup of your team, especially the management team.

Minorities' representation (or lack thereof) at the top speaks volumes about the culture of an organization. Plus, when a candidate or a minority team member does not see someone who looks like them at or near the top of the organization, it tells them that their opportunity for upper mobility is limited. They may choose to advance their careers somewhere else.

What About Inclusion?

Building a diverse team is one thing, but it does not mean they have a voice or that you value their contributions and unique perspectives.

For your company to be considered inclusive, you must ensure the safety and well-being of all your employees, use inclusive language, offer flexible-work options and parental leave, celebrate diverse holidays, and accommodate observance of religious needs.

Much like I did when my kids attended the JCC preschool, leaders must ask, *What is acceptable? What isn't? What do I need to do? What is appropriate?*

Great leaders ensure people are comfortable representing their culture or their faith. They inquire about minorities' needs and are proactive about offering an opportunity for employees to voice their concerns and opinions without the fear of victimization.

Engage and Learn

If you're committed to making a difference, **encourage conversations** among your team members to help them understand and value diversity and inclusion. Think of it as the dinner table conversation with your kids. Make it casual and devoid of judgment. Discuss unconscious biases. You may want to start by sharing your own and, in doing so, promote self-awareness.

Again, admitting and sharing your own shortcomings will, at a very minimum, encourage others to do some self-reflection. You may provide tools like Harvard's Implicit Association Test. This online test is a great way to identify your and your team's unconscious biases.

Don't stop there. **Encourage interactions**. When we hosted guests from Japan, Nigeria, South Africa, Morocco, and several Hispanic cultures, and when we had Muslims, Jews, and same-sex couples at our home, we sent a clear message to our kids that embracing diversity is a lot more than just talking about it. It means including them in our lives.

Meet People Halfway

I cannot pretend to truly understand the feelings or experiences of people who are being discriminated against because of the color of their skin, religious beliefs, or sexual orientation. But I *can* talk about discrimination from the perspective of a woman in a male-dominated world.

Women face countless obstacles in the workplace just by being women. This includes facing societal pressure to give up a career for the sake of kids. Why should being a mom and having a career be mutually exclusive for women but not for men?

I can talk about the misogyny women encounter and the assumptions some men make about women in leadership. I have seen female representation dwindle the closer you get to the top of organizations. And I have seen companies promote men on the base of their *potential*, while they wouldn't consider women applying for the same position, citing their *lack of experience.*

Likewise, I have seen men apply for jobs that they were nowhere near qualified for while accomplished women doubted their abilities despite their experience.

I can attest to the higher standards women have to live up to especially when it comes to their physical appearances.

However, just because I'm part of one minority doesn't mean I understand the marginalization of other minorities. I am treading with caution here, but I believe minorities can and should vigorously engage in the conversation and do work of their own.

Help others understand your needs and do so without judgment. I believe some of us are reluctant to engage with some minorities because *we just don't know how.* We are afraid of making faux pas or hurting someone's feelings.

Rather than waiting for people to ask questions, start the conversation and help them understand a few things. This will open the door to a two-way conversation.

Be prepared for their mistakes and help them recover. Explain what is and isn't appropriate and what is offensive—just like my friend Marcy was clear about all I needed to know about Jewish culture, saving me from a few cultural blunders.

I remember attending a bat mitzvah years ago for a friend of Margot's. When Dan and I were introduced to the rabbi, I extended my hand. He looked at me but did not return the handshake. After an awkward pause, his wife stepped up and shook my hand instead.

What I didn't know was that this was an orthodox rabbi. He wasn't allowed to have physical contact with a woman other than his wife. She had come to my rescue and prevented me from being left hanging, clueless, and mortified. Her perceptiveness made a big difference. She realized I did not know any better, and she didn't make me feel judged because of it.

——

We're a long way away from living in a perfect society, but I have faith in the younger generation who are growing up in a deeply connected and wide-open world.

Diversity has become a competitive differentiator that positively impacts performance and attracts talent. Statistically, companies that are more diverse clearly outperform other companies. So diversity and inclusion are not only *the right thing to do*, but it's also *the smart thing to do*. If for no other reason, an inclusive workforce helps bring your organization closer to the people you are trying to appeal to, whether future team members or clients.

22
Merci, Maman!

———

I f you look up *nurture* in the thesaurus, you'll find words like *care, develop, cultivate, support, foster, encourage, promote, stimulate, boost, assist, advance, help,* and *strengthen.*

While they are usually associated with mothers, these behaviors should be expected of leaders. Isn't developing team members and guiding them toward a goal the same as providing care and attention to children so they can grow up to reach the best of their abilities?

Fortunately, top-down styles of leadership have become archaic, and younger generations have little tolerance for such authoritative leaders. Instead, the most effective way to lead is through relationships based on care, mutual respect, empowerment, and engagement.

This does not mean that leadership is all rainbows and unicorns. Nor is motherhood, for that matter. Both roles are hard and frustrating at times as you find out that there is only so much you can do. You can create the right family environment for your kids to thrive, but you still don't know for sure whether you're saving for college tuition or for bail money.

Likewise, leaders can demonstrate all the right behaviors to have a great team culture, but it's like saying, "Let's have fun!" You cannot *make* people have fun. But you can create the right environment hoping that they do.

Leaders and mothers alike hope that the seeds they planted, the resources they invested, and the time they committed will bloom and turn into the ambitious vision they have set out, one where people thrive.

When it comes to effective leadership, you don't need a magic wand, nor do you need Pixie Dust. Just apply all the basic principles described in this book: teach, train, set expectations, encourage, coach and correct, and model behavior. Then rinse and repeat. That's what moms try to do day in and day out.

I wrote this book hoping to help leaders who are looking for answers and inspiration. When you feel stuck, plagued by doubt, second-guessing, and pressured to make the right decisions, ask yourself, *What would I do if these team members were my kids?* The answer you're looking for may be right there, staring you in the face.

> "In doubt, go back to basics. The best solutions are often the simple ones."
> Nouha to Katia
> Los Angeles, CA, USA

I also wrote this book for stay-at-home moms and dads who are doubting their ability to reenter the workforce and take on leadership responsibilities. Let me remind you: You know more than you think. If you have mastered the art of calming a toddler, have learned to multitask through the school years, and have survived raising a teenager, you're ready to lead a team.

In the end, remember that you were a child once. You *know how it feels* when parenting is effective and when it isn't. You can probably remember the times when you took advantage of your mom's mistakes and escaped the grips of accountability. I certainly can.

Indeed, mothers are a great source of wisdom when it comes to leadership. And even though they don't always get it right, they still teach children what works and what doesn't.

There's no doubt that mothers do the best and possibly the hardest job in the world while providing an endless supply of love *and* tough love . . . and though they do not get any form of compensation, they have gifted us one more thing—the basic principles of great leadership.

So if you haven't done so yet, take a moment to appreciate and thank your mom for her hard work and for what she has given you—lessons in life . . . and in leadership.

POSTSCRIPT

B ack in the eighties, had you asked me how I envisioned my life, I would have answered without a shadow of a doubt that I wanted a career and had no interest in getting married, much less having children. Well, not only did I get married, I have not one, not two, but *three* wonderful kids.

I don't know what I did to deserve these three children, but they are kind, funny, healthy, and hard-working. I consider other qualities icing on the cake. I know this probably oozes motherly bias, but I feel lucky to have been granted these three incredible individuals—not only because of their great personalities but also because they are so different from one another.

It never ceases to amaze me that the same two parents can have three such different children, each with a particular set of skills, talents, and a distinct personality. I guess this reality is meant to keep parents on their toes. With each child, we have to come up with a customized strategy.

As a mother, the very act of releasing a human being from your body gives you an entirely new perspective on life. It also gives you new priorities. In raising that tiny human, you also become more resilient and more patient. The beauty of it is that you keep learning through the process. Having kids educates you in unexpected ways. Looking back, I recognize that my kids may have taught me as much as I have taught them.

Jullian, Margot, and Tristan: Thank you for teaching me so much. I cherish every lesson. I treasure every insight. I welcome all the knowledge you continue to share with me.

I love you. Always.

Maman

OVER TO YOU

trust that reading *Manage Like a Mother* has helped you identify some opportunities to grow as a leader. Below are some questions that can further help illuminate potential blind spots.

You may use these to guide you in applying a mother's wisdom to your role as a leader in any organization, big or small.

For a printable version, please visit Cockerellconsulting.com/ManageLikeAMother

1. Character Matters—*Hiring for Values*

- What do I value most as a leader? Which behaviors support these values?
- What are the nonnegotiable values and behaviors I expect from my team members?
- How do I communicate my organization's values to applicants?

2. Welcome Aboard—*Orientation 101*

- What is our current onboarding process?
- What evidence is there that my organization cares about new employees? Are the new hires' arrival a priority? Do we make recruits feel welcome?

- Is there a process in place to get to know our new team members?

3. Teach Them Their ABCs—*Effective Training*

- Which learning styles do we incorporate in our training program?
- Do we provide new team members with the opportunity to ask questions and extend their training, if necessary? When do we do so?
- How do we ensure new team members are ready to operate independently?
- Do we currently have a process in place to evaluate the quality of our training program? If so, does it include the following questions?
  - » What roadblocks have you encountered?
  - » What do you wish you had known about the job?
  - » Is there an area you wish you had known more about?
  - » What could we do differently as an organization?
  - » How can we better prepare for future new hires?
  - » Who and what was most helpful through your onboarding and training process?

4. You've Got a Friend in Me—*Building Strong Relationships*

- As a leader, what is the quality of my relationship with my team members?
- Thinking about each of my direct reports, how well can I answer the following questions?
  - » What does this person need to relax and recharge?
  - » How does this person arrive at decisions or reach conclusions?

» Is this person thorough and methodical in their approach?

» Does this person shine in group settings, or do they tend to talk only when prompted?

» Does this person like to be praised publicly, or do they prefer to be acknowledged in private?

» How does this person respond to change and last-minute requests?

5. Listening Ears and an Understanding Heart—*Emotional Intelligence*

• What generally triggers my emotional reactions?

• How can I ensure I express my emotions appropriately?

• What should I do to show I recognize the feelings of others?

• Do I regularly pay attention to the following:

» Has there been a change lately in team members' individual performance and behavior?

» Are some team members more flustered or seem more overwhelmed than usual?

» Do they sulk or demonstrate hostility through their body language?

» Are they quick to present a rebuttal?

» Do I sense disinterest and distraction?

» What might be the root of these behaviors?

• How often do I ask the following questions of individual team members:

» Is your workload manageable and are deadlines realistic?

» How can I help resolve the recurring issues that are stressing you and causing you to feel overwhelmed?

» How can I help make your work experience better?

6. Because I Said So—*Setting Expectations*

- How often does my team deliver results that do not meet my expectations? Were expectations laid out clearly?
- What are the individual skills of those on my team?
  - » What are the skills required for this specific Have you ever considered leaving the organization? If so, what prompted it? Did this happen recently?
- Am I matching task to talent?
- What are the resources available to my team? What are the resources required? Am I matching task to resources?
- Do I provide a specific date and time for the completion of tasks?

7. What Might Be—*Casting a Long-Term Vision*

- As an organization and a team, what are we trying to achieve in the five- to ten-year range?
- How do I communicate this long-term vision to my organization? And with what frequency?
- Daily, what do we do to achieve this long-term goal?
- Do we have a clear strategy to achieve our vision?

8. Trust in Me—*Creating an Environment of Trust*

- How can I better demonstrate my values and priorities through my behaviors?
- How do I hold myself accountable to my team?
- Which responsibilities can I delegate to my team members and show that I trust their judgment?
- How can I share the spotlight with peers or team members?
- Do I tend to say negative things about others?

When Dealing with a Breach of Trust
- Were there signs I may be trusting this person too quickly? Did I fail to see the writing on the wall?
- Does this breach of trust reflect the character of the individual?
- Does the person demonstrate genuine concern? Do they understand why I am feeling the way I do?
- Does this person appear to be willing to change their behavior?
- How can we move on and collaborate in the future?
- Are there new rules I can put in place so we can trust each other once again?

9. Dispensing Tough Love—*Giving Feedback*
- How can I better prepare to give effective feedback?
- What am I afraid of?
- How will the feedback be received?
- Have I set the correct expectations in the first place?
- What is the behavior I am trying to correct?
- What are the facts I can rely on?
- How does this behavior affect the team and the organization?
- What will happen if I don't deliver the feedback?

After Delivering Feedback
- Did I provide the team member an opportunity to express their point of view?
- Did I encourage the team member to offer a resolution or a course of action?
- What follow-up do we need? Did I set a timeline or due date?

10. Bravos and Encores—*Rewards and Recognition*

- What process do I currently have in place to provide rewards and recognition to my team?
- How can I ensure recognition is focused on both efforts *and* results?
- Which behaviors do I hope to see become second nature in the organization?
- How do my individual team members respond to rewards and recognition? Do I know their personal preference when it comes to being recognized?

11. Can You Hear Me Now?—*Effective Communication*

- What are my specific communication protocols to reach different individuals or groups within the company? (e.g., in-person communication, meeting, memo, one-on-one, town hall, podcast, voice mail?)
- For each group I work with, which method of communication would be most effective? (e.g., in-person communication, meeting, memo, one-on-one, town hall, podcast, voice mail . . .)
- Is there an opportunity for me to create an information hub? Who should be the team members assigned to communicating information to their side of the organization?
- What can I do to improve the effectiveness of meetings? (e.g., purpose, attendees, time, agenda)
- Which meetings can I move from a meeting room to a walking meeting?
- What mechanisms have I put in place to let the flow of information come back to me?
- How will I make myself more approachable and accessible?

- How can I be more visible in the operation?
- How frequently should I host office hours during which I am available to my team members?
- How can team members reach me anonymously?
- What is the most effective way for my team to reach me? Have I set a timeline for my responses?
- How frequently should I host team feedback sessions?
- How do I react when presented with bad news or negative feedback?

12. Once Upon a Time . . .—*Storytelling as a Leadership Practice*

- When can I use storytelling as a leadership practice?
- Which stories would capture the essence of the values and culture of my organization?
- What changes do I hope to see as a result of sharing these stories?
- What do I need to do to improve my storytelling ability?

13. I Want to Be Like You—*Being a Role Model*

- What are the most important behaviors I can model for my team?
- What are specific moments I can create to model behaviors?
- How can I better model vulnerability?
- What behaviors can I model to new hires to make a lasting first impression?
- How can my team and I call out discrepancies, i.e., saying one thing and doing another?

14. It's About Time!—*Time Management*

- Which repetitive tasks on my list can I bundle together?

- Which task can I break into more manageable assignments?
- How can I decrease distractions and interruptions?
- How can I create a plan of action to fight procrastination?
- How can I prioritize the most important tasks and let go of the less important ones?
- Who are the individuals I can rely on? What task may I be able to delegate to them?
- How will I commit to creating a daily plan of action?
- Weekly, how much time will I dedicate to myself?
- Monthly, how much time will I set aside to address long-term goals?

15. Where There's a Will, There's a Way—*Problem-Solving through Creative Thinking*

- How can I build an environment where it is safe to voice ideas?
- How often should I host brainstorming and problem-solving sessions?
- How do I communicate that failure is acceptable in the quest for innovation and problem-solving?
- How should I celebrate the problem-solving and creative process?

16. Plays Well with Others—*Collaboration*

- How can I make my team aware of each other's skills, strengths, and talents?
- How can I position my leaders to become teachers in their field of expertise?
- What can I do to reward collaboration when I see it?

- When rating a team member, do I consider the following questions?
  - » Does this person welcome others' input?
  - » Is this person non-judgmental and open-minded?
  - » Does this person keep others informed?
  - » Does this person support others and provide them with constructive feedback?
  - » Does this person prioritize group efforts toward a common goal?
  - » Does this person leverage the talents, skills, and abilities of others?
  - » Does this person celebrate the achievements of others?

17. Can't You Just Get Along?—*Conflict Management*
- When managing conflict, what do I need to do to ensure the best outcome possible?
- How can I ensure we quickly go from pointing fingers to finding solutions?
- Where can we find common ground?
- What is the common goal my team can rally around?

18. Navigating the Rapids—*Dealing with Crisis Situations*
- When dealing with a crisis, how can I improve my ability to assess the situation?
- What do I need to do to ensure confidence is quickly restored?

19. Just Keep Learning—*Personal Development*
- With what frequency should I dedicate time to growing my skills?

- How often do I encourage my team to share their knowledge with me?
- How do I ensure I learn from my mistakes?
- What self-development goals can I set for myself?

20. Where Do Babies Come From?—*Fostering Curiosity*

- When and where can I encourage my team to share what they know or have recently learned?
- How can I encourage inquisitiveness from my team?
- How can I lead a conversation with questions and encourage my team's input?
- What questions should I ask to spark curiosity?

21. What a Wonderful World—*Diversity*

- How diverse is my current team?
- What changes should we make in our selection process to create a more diverse pool of candidates?
- How can I develop self-awareness and identify my unconscious bias?
- How can I become more purposeful in discussing diversity with my team?
- How can I encourage minority team members to teach others?
- How can I encourage inclusiveness in my organization?

22. Merci, Maman!—*Conclusion*

- What specific behaviors did I learn from my mom?

ACKNOWLEDGMENTS

This book has been many years in the making. The initial idea started with my father-in-law, Lee, who often talks about his mom and how she influenced him becoming the outstanding leader he is today. Though he and I were raised at different times and on different continents, I could relate to many of the experiences he shared.

Once I had children of my own, I realized the lessons taught by a mother are not only timeless, but they also transfer from one generation to the next, one family to another, and eventually that they could be applied to the workplace. That is all the motivation I needed for this book.

Many people helped me put these ideas on paper.

My editor, Adele Booysen, not only corrected my sometimes-hazy English grammar but also pushed me to crystallize my thoughts when I found myself somewhat lost in translation.

Karen Anderson and David Hancock at Morgan James Publishing agreed to publish my book. I am so very grateful for their vote of confidence.

Of course, I must thank my friends and family from around the world who readily contributed their favorite quotes from their mothers. I am so grateful for their love and friendship which proves that we never grow apart from the people we love, no matter the time or the distance.

To all the hard-working parents I know, thank you for inspiring me. As parents, we may not always be perfect, but our hearts are always in the right place.

To Lee and Priscilla, the best in-laws I could hope for, and to the rest of my American family: Thank you for welcoming me in what is now my home away from home and for accepting me with open arms into your clan. (Sorry about that Thanksgiving couscous!)

To my sister Annick, my brother-in-law Eric, my nieces and nephew, and my entire family in France, you may be far but always on my mind.

To my mom, Anna, you're simply the best.

To my husband Dan. Thank you for being my Honey Bunny. I am forever your Lemon Pie.

ABOUT THE AUTHOR

Valerie was born and raised in France, where she graduated with a degree in business hospitality. In 1987/88, she participated in Epcot's World Showcase Fellowship program at Walt Disney World. Upon returning to France, she took a job in a bank as an investment advisor.

In 1991, Valerie was hired by Disneyland Paris as a retail manager and ran multiple merchandise locations in the Resort Division. That year, she traveled to the US for training and met Dan, who was also working on the Disney management team. The two got married in 1993. Valerie eventually joined the Merchandise Buying Office and oversaw the assortment planning for all resort merchandise locations at Disneyland Paris.

Valerie and her husband relocated to Florida in 1997. She pursued her career in retail at Walt Disney World and oversaw assortments for Downtown Disney, Epcot, and the Disney Cruise Line. Valerie left the company to raise her three children—Jullian,

Margot, and Tristan—and she later started consulting for outside organizations in the retail world.

She returned to Disney in 2013 to become a contract facilitator for the Disney Institute. Valerie facilitated professional development classes and custom programs in both French and English. She drew from her international management experience in retail and operations to teach Disney's approach to Leadership Excellence and Customer Service.

In May 2019, Valerie joined Dan in creating Cockerell Consulting. They facilitate workshops around the US and the world. During these workshops as well as through her coaching work and speaking engagements, Valerie shares her expertise in building a great culture in organizations and leadership excellence. She hopes to inspire women in particular to take on more leadership responsibilities and reach their full potential.

For inquiries, questions or comments, Valerie can be reached at CockerellConsulting.com.

A free ebook edition is available with the purchase of this book.

To claim your free ebook edition:

1. Visit MorganJamesBOGO.com
2. Sign your name CLEARLY in the space
3. Complete the form and submit a photo of the entire copyright page
4. You or your friend can download the ebook to your preferred device

A **FREE** ebook edition is available for you or a friend with the purchase of this print book.

CLEARLY SIGN YOUR NAME ABOVE

Instructions to claim your free ebook edition:
1. Visit MorganJamesBOGO.com
2. Sign your name CLEARLY in the space above
3. Complete the form and submit a photo of this entire page
4. You or your friend can download the ebook to your preferred device

Print & Digital Together Forever.

Snap a photo

Free ebook

Read anywhere

Printed in the USA
CPSIA information can be obtained
at www.ICGtesting.com
JSHW020924020923
47734JS00002B/27